The Secrets of
ATTRACTION

MARTIN LLOYD-ELLIOTT

The Secrets of
ATTRACTION

Decoding body language to maximize
your sex appeal

LONDON NEW YORK SYDNEY TORONTO

PHOTOGRAPHY BY COLIN GOTTS

This edition published in Great Britain in 1994
by BCA by arrangement with
Reed Consumer Books Ltd
Michelin House, 81 Fulham Road
London SW3 6RB

CN 3518

Produced by Mandarin Offset
Printed in Hong Kong

DEDICATION

I dedicate this book to all my friends in psychology and psychotherapy, especially Simone Warner, Gloria Litman, Françoise Golden, Michael Perring, Caroline Herbert, Jacob Zelinger, Andy Evans, George Sik and Brian Tully, whose combined endless talents, and enthusiasm in the search for truth and understanding of the human mind, never cease to give me inspiration. Together they have taught me that the way to hope is through searing introspection, the unconditional non-judgemental love of our fellow beings and the undertaking to use the power of psychology for good and positive change.

NOTE *The contents of this book are based on personal observations of human interaction and on numerous scientific research projects. Despite the obvious existence of distinct behavioural patterns and courtship rituals it should be noted that all human beings are individuals and that every transpersonal interaction is a unique event requiring thoughtful consideration and the application of courtesy and common sense.*

CONTENTS

INTRODUCTION

It is 1924, and you are at the picture house with your date. The lights dim and on the screen the flickering silent images tell their unambiguous tale of drama and romance. The villain – easily identifiable as he looks like a villain and pulls the facial expressions of a villain – cavorts in a dastardly fashion, while the outraged heroine's father gasps at the prospect of his daughter's marriage to the tall dark handsome stranger, the hero. He is immediately recognizable, too, as he walks like a hero, wears his clothes like a hero, and smiles a smile to make every girl in the audience experience a mild heart flutter.

As for the heroine, her eyes are to die for. She glances sideways from the screen, head tilted slightly to one side, flutters her eyelashes outrageously, looks at once hopelessly vulnerable and disconcertingly inviting, and each man in the audience feels that she has chosen him.

In the darkness, your date edges a tenth of an inch closer to you, yet even this tiny movement you detect. Your personal radar, which is turned to maximum sensitivity because you are so mutually attracted, can even tell when his eyes steal a momentary glance in your direction, even though his face stays rigidly turned towards the screen. You are desperate to look at his face too but you do not want to be seen to do so. When you are sure he is not looking you turn your eyes towards him. For an eternal moment you are transfixed, blood beating in your ears, as he continues to look away – though he is fully aware that your eyes are upon him. Then, ever so gently, you allow your right foot to ease closer to his left foot. If he moves his foot back towards you, your feet must surely touch. The anticipation is electric. You touch feet, ever so gently. The contact is made and in the innocence of the encounter your minds conjure up visions of passionate kissing. And all this without a word. You have known exactly what was going on in the film without hearing a single word of dialogue. You also know intuitively when and how to move closer, how to read the signals between you with accurate clarity. You are a master of the body language of seduction.

If only it was so easy! Drag yourself away from this rose-spectacled fantasy into the present and a lively informal party. There are about twenty-five people scattered about the room; some are eating and talking in small groups, some are obviously couples. One young pair seem oblivious of everyone, gazing as if hypnotised into each other's eyes. Another couple sit so close on the sofa that their intimate mutual proximity makes it clear at once that they are lovers. But of the rest few are demonstrating unequivocally that they are unapproachable.

Some of the men are dressed quite formally, others very casually. Some have short hair, others long, one a beard. All provoke assumptions based on their appearance. The women are equally diverse; one wears a provocatively short

INTRODUCTION

Left: A momentary exchange of glances opens a non-verbal dialogue loaded with sexual potential. Having held each other's gaze for a second they pretend to continue reading. In fact they feel the charged excitement that fills the air as a consequence of their intense mutual attraction. For the exchange to continue they must reestablish eye contact. When this happens perhaps one of them will indicate a desire to move closer.

dress, another has a plunging neckline. Some are 'power' dressers, while others are anonymous. From the colour and style of our hair, to the fashion of our shoes, we all make dramatic non-verbal statements about ourselves. Inevitably such assumptions that people initially draw will be inaccurate but it is not just our style of clothing and physical appearance that influence our non-verbal communication. Numerous other factors come into play. Our body postures and gestures speak volumes; insensitivity to such signals can lead to crushingly embarrassing situations. For example, at this party the door suddenly swings open and a cowboy-type character struts into the room running his hands through his hair, 501's too tightly stretched over his behind. He has on half a gallon of cheap aftershave and has already had a few drinks. He makes straight for the food. He reckons he is the sexiest hunk in the place and knows he is going to get lucky. After a few bites he scans the room and spots a tall, very attractive woman. She is with a group of other women but he only has eyes for her. She has noticed him, of course, and has nudged one of her friends, who has also now sneaked a glance at him. They laugh behind their hands and her friend rolls her eyes. 'Oh, magic,' the poor man thinks enthusiastically to himself, 'she likes me . . . in fact I bet she fancies the hell out of me'.

Meanwhile, from where the women stand, things look a little different. 'God, look at that prat staring at me,' Anna says to her friend Shelley. 'Which one?' Shelley asks. 'Him, look at that idiot with the leather jacket and the popping eyes.' Oh Anna, he's disgusting! Oh no, he's coming over.'

He is not put off in the slightest when they turn to face away from him. On the contrary, being the eternal optimist, he interprets the women's behaviour as a come-on. He stumbles blindly on like a robot, arrives at their reversed defensive wall and blunders even deeper in to what is inevitably going to become a humiliating experience. He attempts to squeeze between two touching shoulders then tries to slide a hand through at waist level, completely oblivious to the non-verbal, non-sexual signals being fired at him in great volleys. The women's turned backs, crossed arms protecting their breasts, their annoyed and slightly anxious looks, lack of eye contact except for occasional dagger stares and their glances round the room in the hope of establishing eye contact with a potential rescuer are all obvious signals of rejection.

Across the other side of the room, Michael – average looks, average height, nothing flash, has been observing the saga unfold. He too was struck by Anna's looks but decided to read the situation more carefully. So far he has been listening very attentively, so he knows her name, some of her interests, and what she does at work. A couple of times in the last ten minutes their eyes have met and the last time they both smiled just for a second. Now several other people are blocking the eye contact channel between them, so Michael moves across the room to the other side of her friends, bringing him once again into Anna's line of vision. He sees that she is being pestered and moves forward. Without a word he waits, willing Anna to look towards him. Her eyes are searching the room, hoping to see the gentle smile she had encountered earlier. When their eyes meet across the room she cannot stop herself looking relieved and pleased. He gestures with a nod towards the area of the room where people are dancing and she accepts with a minute, unconscious shrug of her shoulders and an affirming smile and nod. They begin to dance together, although as yet neither of them has said a single word. Meanwhile, Anna's girlfriends move away from the man as if he were infectious, leaving him alone and confused – all because his body language is hopeless, insensitive and unsexy. Such situations are sadly all too familiar to many of us, but avoiding such obvious non-verbal blunders forms only part of the answer. Whatever circumstances we find ourselves in, we always act as amateur psychologists trying to analyse other peoples' behaviour and thoughts and to read situations, and never more so than in potentially romantic encounters.

This book is to help people understand sexual body language by awakening the instinctive knowledge that often lies dormant in the the unconscious. We signal a dozen things without words for every message that is delivered in spoken language. Some researchers have suggested that 65 per cent of our communication is non-verbal, others put it as high as 80 per cent or even 93 per cent.

It is a complicated business: Mario Pei claims to have identified 700,000 different human non-verbal signals and another researcher, M. H. Krout, reported 5000 individual hand gestures with verbal equivalents. This book on body language will have inevitable shortfalls because profound or detailed academic debate about research methodologies etc. has been avoided. Nevertheless, here at last is the first specialized book about body language and the secrets of attraction, designed to help you to greater success in your search for love.

HUMANS AND SEX

We humans are such sexual beings. Sex is a principal motivator in our lives. Beyond the short-term gratification of great sex, which sadly is often not achieved, lies the much greater and universally shared longing for love. How we set about searching for another person to love and be loved by often occupies a great amount of our thinking time while awake, day-dreaming, and even our dreams while asleep. Many people make mistakes in their search for love much of the time, and these failures and often heartbreaking misunderstandings usually

occur because we have failed to comprehend or perhaps even think about the non-verbal signals that we are sending out to others and receiving back from those around us. It is possible to change, but it may require some uncomfortable searing self-searching in order to increase your self-awareness, and ultimately improve your self-confidence. In addition, it will take some really committed hard work, both at home and out in 'the research field' with other people, to properly study this subject and develop new 'reading skills' with sensitivity, accuracy and sincerity.

However, with patience and practice you will be able to tell if another person is available for a potential encounter; if they are interested in talking to you, dancing with you or even kissing you; you will be able to understand why men seem so hopeless at picking up apparently clear signals of 'yes' or 'no' or 'I haven't decided yet' and why a woman who is really interested in a man may: a) avoid him like the plague, b) look away every time he smiles at her, c) hardly eat anything at all the first time he takes her for a feast at his favourite restaurant.

So men, next time you find yourself thinking, 'It's so embarrassing, I don't know why she doesn't take the hint, I thought I'd made it so obvious I am just not interested' or 'I fancy her so much, yet she doesn't seem to even notice me. I don't dare risk asking her out for a date as I would be so humiliated if she said no' or 'Every time I try and chat up a girl at a party it's total disaster and I don't know why', reach for this book. It should help.

And female readers, if you identify with any of the following thoughts, you'll find the information you need in this book: 'I'm going steady with my boyfriend and I'm not interested in having a fling with anyone else. Every time I go out with my girlfriends for a drink I get constant hassle from men who think I'm interested in them and who get angry when I end up having to shout at them that I'm just not interested. If only I could put them off without having to say a word' or 'OK, yes, I do like him but how do I show him without coming on too strong. I don't want to seem too easy, but I don't want him to ignore me because he thinks I'm not interested. And then I don't even know what he's thinking about me. I wish people didn't play so many games. I wish I knew how to read him so I could tell if it was going the way I hope it is.'

Understand the secrets of sexual body language and quickly you will know far more about what other people are thinking – thoughts they may or may not wish you to know; feelings they may not yet have consciously realized for themselves.

This text is going to embark upon a comprehensive study of this exciting subject area, first by looking at principal factors that affect our body language, namely our developmental history, the environment, the context and our individual needs for space around us; then, in Chapter 2, it will examine the central issue of 'leakage', that is, the non-verbal signals that slip out without us realizing, revealing our hidden thoughts often against our wishes; then Chapter 3 looks at first impressions and how important they are. Chapter 4 examines the whole subject of aesthetics: what and whom we find attractive and why, and what we can do to enhance our best assets, with a special section on honesty and dishonesty and the give-away signals that help us sort the truth tellers from the liars.

Next, the book takes you on a grand tour of the body from the top of the head to the tips of the toes. Every bit of us expresses our thoughts.

Finally the book looks at the multi-layered world of complex gesture clusters, what we find most in real-life encounters, where people send numerous individual non-verbal communications simultaneously. The skill to be learnt is how to interpret complex and perhaps contradictory signals. By the last chapter the reader will know a myriad secrets about the body language of attraction.

But first, let us look at the development of our sexuality and how this might affect our sexual body language.

THE DEVELOPMENT OF SEXUAL NON-VERBAL COMMUNICATION SKILLS

How sexually connected we are with our bodies may be linked with our own personal sexual development. Most of us become aware of the sexual pleasure potential of our bodies through masturbation. Boys tend to touch themselves and masturbate from a very young age. Their genitals are of course very obvious and easily accessible. Male sexual arousal is very focused on the penis, and nearly all men are adept at making themselves come for sexual gratification by the age of 15. For most men, therefore, the concept of love-making is formed in direct relation to their experience of masturbation.

Women's early teenage sexual experience often excludes masturbation, enabling their bodies to emerge as sensitive and sensual without their sexual awareness being focused exclusively on the genitals. A woman's skin is actually more sensitive than a man's, but a woman seems also more able to gain significant sexual arousal from all areas of her body, not just the obviously erogenous ones. Thus in non-verbal sexual signalling a woman is more aware, even if subconsciously, of the subtle potential in each and every part of her body, and this will be displayed in the signals she sends.

This difference between the sexes may explain why males are so apparently bad at non-verbal sexual communication in comparison to their female counter-

parts. Men do have much to learn from women in this area. They do not need to become effeminate in their body language (although a degree of femininity does act as a strong turn-on for some women) but rather understand that, by watching and learning from women's non-verbal dialogues and by incorporating some of these sentences into their own non-verbal vocabulary, they will speak the language more competently, be more attractive to women and potentially become much more skilled lovers too. However, this does not mean that all women are natural experts in this field. Many women are unaware of the sexual signals they send, or are unfamiliar with the complexities of non-verbal skills.

This book aims to help you build on the knowledge and skills that you already possess. It is not intended to help trick people into bed, or to manipulate people against their will; any relationship based on dishonesty or exploitation will serve only to cause you and others great hurt. Psychology is a really exciting area of science which has the potential to bring the joy of self-discovery and greater understanding into all of our lives. Used well, a knowledge of psychology can enhance your life and that of those around you. It can relieve distress and anxiety and empower you to become a more sensitive, confident and successful person in your relationships with others.

The knowledge contained in this book will not give you any magic powers. You do not need magic, as you already have at your disposal a fabulous array of senses, each one of which you are probably using at half capacity or less: sight, taste, touch, hearing and smell, and then of course, your sixth sense, your radar, intuition, gut reaction – call it what you will. All these have a great role to play in building your talents when it comes to the art of attraction without words.

The first and most important secret in the success of understanding sexual body language is honesty. Honesty with yourself and other people is the key to enlightenment and happiness. It is pointless pretending to be something or someone that we are not in order to successfully seduce someone because, if the ploy succeeds, the relationship is based on a false premise and ultimately it will fail.

In an age where the risk of infection with a deadly sexually transmitted disease forces us to exercise great caution before entering upon fully blown sexual encounters, and at a time when so many relationships end in great sadness and recrimination, the observations in this text will, I hope, help people to be more sensitive to the amazing world of non-verbal communication, particularly when it applies to one of the central motivators of our existence – love and sex.

CHAPTER ONE

PERSONAL SPACE ZONES

Human beings are very aware of their surroundings. All of our senses make our species adept at monitoring events taking place in the environment, ranging from sensing vibrations in the ground beneath our feet to developing a pre-thunderstorm headache even before black clouds gather overhead. Our senses are the key to the survival of our race. We can detect potentially harmful objects approaching us at speed,

and can take immediate avoiding action. We can smell when food is unfit to eat and can detect the subtlest changes in body odour. Both men and women can sense when someone out of their line of vision is staring at them and can be aware of the close proximity of another person even when there is no physical contact. Everyone has the ability to sense another person's vibes or guess at a certain mood. Some people even claim to be able to see the colour of individuals' auras – that is, the energy fields that exist around us.

People who have limited vision or who are completely blind develop an even greater intuitive sense of their immediate surroundings. However, you do not have to have lost your sight to be super-sensitive to objects or other people moving closer to or further away from you. A working knowledge of proxemics – the study of distance between people during communication – is the first prerequisite in enhancing your successful non-verbal sexual communication skills.

Let us start by posing some questions about your attitude to personal space. First, are you an only child? If you are, then you are probably more selfish with your space than someone who has had to share with siblings. You probably still guard your personal space jealously. Secondly, are you an extrovert or introvert? Extroverts tend to allow people to come physically closer to them without experiencing any discomfort.

Above: A courting couple opt to stand within each other's intimate space zone, despite (or perhaps because of) the deserted platform: large empty spaces can be intimidating.
Right: Enforced encroachment leads strangers to arrange themselves so as to touch each other with the least intimate parts of their bodies in an attempt to create the illusion of having a wider, less threatening personal space zone, like an invisible protective bubble.

Thirdly, how tactile are you? Are you someone who hugs close friends and relatives, or was it normal in your family not to touch your parents? Do you find touch easy or stressful? Do you like giving massages and having them done to you, or are you so sensitive that you jump if anyone touches you? Do you dread the first slow dance when you know you might have to come very close to someone else, or do you try to turn a fast dance into a slow one if the other person will give you the chance? How sensitive are you to the touches of others? If you are standing on a crowded train squeezed up against

The shy nature of introverts is reflected in their desire to hold others at least at arm's length and ideally to keep people far enough away from them to be able to literally keep an eye on the whole person. Extroverts tend to seek out the company of others and enjoy the close proximity that companionship often brings; their inclination is to move in closer to people. Thus if an extrovert is attracted towards an introvert there will follow an absurd unconscious dance, as every time the extrovert closes in on the introvert's territory the latter will take a step backwards. The extrovert may well interpret this as a 'come on' and take another step closer, and so on.

Above: Strangers stuck in a broken-down lift position themselves as far apart as possible in the attempt to create the illusion of greater space around each other, avoiding eye contact and guarding their intimate space zones with protective arms and hands. At first they avoid any interaction.

Right: Some time later, the man attempts to chat up one of his fellow passengers but in doing so invades her intimate space zone, causing discomfort, indicated by her leaning away from him, her defensive arm position and her facial displeasure. The other passenger squeezes herself anxiously into the corner.

four or five other people are you very conscious of which bits of you are touching or are you oblivious to the physical contact? Your personal level of tactile tolerance or enjoyment will affect how aroused you become when others move into close proximity with you. Your brain has a choice of emotional responses to metabolic arousal. Which feeling you choose – fear, anger, pleasure – will be influenced by the circumstances of the interaction; the sex of the people crowding you; your age; your personality; your nationality; where you live; and how intimate your relationship is with the other person.

The people we are prepared to welcome into the very intimate air space around our bodies are those to whom we are closely bonded. It requires a high degree of trust to let anyone come so close as to be able to touch any part of our body with any part of theirs! People who live in crowded cities are generally more tolerant of having to share their physical space with other people than rural dwellers. This has important consequences for interactions of a potentially intimate nature: a country person will perceive the city dweller's automatic urge to stand in close proximity during conversation as rude or even threatening. Be sensitive to people's need for personal space. If they step back when you approach them it does not automatically mean they are not attracted to you; they just need more space to feel comfortable. It is vital that a person to whom you are attracted is able to feel comfortable in any exchange, otherwise any potential mutual attraction they might feel will be overridden by their automatic desire to adhere to their normal spatial rules.

Above: The two women take refuge in the safety of each other's intimate space zone, normally reserved for close friends, family or lovers. Their two pairs of folded arms create a defensive wall that send a clear signal to the man, who is left in the farthest corner, his arms folded and head down, indicating his withdrawal from any attempt to communicate.

Cultural differences are significant when it comes to personal space zones. How much space people require in order to feel comfortable relates directly to how much they touch each other, non-sexually, during conversation. People from Spain, Portugal, Italy and Greece all touch quite a lot and therefore stand within easy touching distance when with friends. People from Latin America and the Middle East tend to touch even more and enjoy standing very close during verbal or non-verbal exchanges. On the other hand the North Americans, British, most Northern Europeans and Australians react generally very negatively if you come too close. You should always take the cultural background of people into consideration and avoid the supposition that what feels good for you must also feel good for them. The saying 'when in Rome, do as the Romans do' has significant implications for the student of non-verbal sexual communication. In one story reported in the psychology literature, a Swedish woman who moved to Australia with her husband was regarded with hostility by local women as a flirt and potential marriage breaker because she had failed to notice that on average Australian women stand seven inches further away from men with whom they are socializing (not flirting) than is the norm in Sweden. Australian women also maintain eye contact with men for a shorter duration than do Swedish women, again leading to a misunderstanding of intent.

Other complex cultural differences abound; for example, although neither the North Americans nor the Japanese touch each other during polite conversation, the Japanese tend to stand much closer to the person to whom they are talking. This leads us to the next influencing factor in proxemics: the sex of the person moving into our personal space. In a meeting between a Japanese woman and an American man, cultural norms would precipitate the Japanese woman moving into the American man's more intimate air space, suggesting to the man a distinct unspoken sexual interest on the part of the woman where none was intended.

Men tend to assume that when a woman moves into their intimate space she is making a sexual move towards them. They immediately begin to

Above: An uninvited invasion of another's personal or intimate space will create a feeling of tension and provoke antagonism. The man's arm reaching around her on the back of the chair, his head and torso pushed forward uncomfortably close to her, and his face brought so close to hers all suggest confrontation. Men are particularly insensitive to the negative consequences of thoughtless space invasion, especially in regard to women.

Right: The woman on the right plays a power game with her work colleague. By sitting on the desk and placing her hand forwards on its surface she is dominating the other's territory. Desks and working areas are an extension of our personal space and their invasion by another can be as unsettling as invasion of our actual personal space. Unspoken and even unconscious emotional rivalries often underlie apparent work-related disputes or challenges for work-place dominance.

imagine a romantic or sexual encounter is developing. If, on the other hand, an American man had sexual designs on a Japanese woman, and moved into her personal space in order to indicate his desire for her, he could mistakenly assume that the fact she did not retreat from him was an indication of her acquiescence. She meanwhile might assume he was just being polite, taking up a typical Japanese man's social space zone.

Within a culture the sex differences are marked. Women tolerate physical invasion of their space by other women to a much higher degree than they accept from men. This is almost certainly because women are encouraged to be much more tactile and physically close to other women during childhood. In contrast, men are very sensitive to other men invading their personal space. They perceive an approach from another man as highly threatening and competitive or else sexual – the latter is perceived as particularly threatening by heterosexual men. When a man moves into another man's personal space uninvited, the consequent state of arousal will be interpreted as fear or anger. When a man moves into a woman's space uninvited, and in the absence of any positive or friendly non-verbal cues, this will be interpreted as threatening. Only an unsolicited invasion of a man's space by a woman is ever positively received, but women should be aware that whatever their intentions may be, their move will be interpreted as a high-scoring non-verbal sexual advance and they should therefore be prepared for the possible consequences. There is a saying, 'If you stand close enough to a man for him to kiss you, he'll probably try.'

Sometimes we are forced by circumstances to allow into our personal space people with whom

Left: Well beyond arm's length, in the social space zone, we feel comfortable in the presence of strangers. However, once eye contact is made, we become very conscious of the distance between us and other people. The artwork is the object of mutual interest and allows for a polite approach. His torso is half-facing the sculpture, suggesting he is non-threatening. She pretends not to be aware of him, but from where she is she can take in his whole 'picture', and assess whether to move into his personal space zone.

we do not wish to have any interaction, let alone a sexual non-verbal dialogue. Under such circumstances we attempt to maintain the illusion of space around us, as can be witnessed clearly in crowded trains or elevators. In this situation we tend to stand very still, tensing our muscles and trying, often without success, to avoid touching anyone else. If forced to touch someone, we attempt to do so with the least sexual parts of our bodies. Shoulders, elbows, clothed arms and backs are all allowed to touch each other. There is a distinct dividing line between permitted and forbidden discomfort. An accidental movement of someone else's

hand into our 'no-go' area will cause us to realign ourselves. We will often employ clothing accessories and bags as token fig leaves to protect our modesty from accidental or deliberate physical contact. Younger people seem generally more tolerant of sharing intimate space with other young people but are as uncomfortable squeezed up against a person from an older generation as are two older people in the same crowded circumstance.

The secret to success in the proxemics dance of love is to arrange yourself to optimum intimate effect in relation to another person's space without causing any discomfort. By its very nature increased

Right: The art gallery provides an ideal setting for a close encounter. As he examines the sculpture closely he touches it, as if to say, 'It feels good, come and see.' She approaches, turning her head slightly on one side in an acknowledgement of his invitation to approach, but still cautiously keeping her distance. However, she has an open body posture with her arms behind her. He lowers his body position by dropping his shoulder, moving his eyes to be on a level with hers.

intimacy is constrained or enhanced by two people's relative proximity. Becoming 'close' to someone emotionally is enacted literally. This is best achieved through an unspoken mutual agreement that you overlap and then merge your touching space zones.

How then does one increase the speed with which the merging of intimate zones occurs? Our culture has developed specific rules about invading and defending personal space. It can become very uncomfortable when either your personal space is invaded by an uninvited intruder, or when you encroach unintentionally too far onto someone else's territory. The secret is to avoid invasion at

comfortable if the man then moves to one side to continue the interaction. Women do not like to be approached from behind or from the side. A man should therefore always avoid sitting or standing alongside a woman to whom he wishes to display his interest and attraction. It is much easier to flirt across a dinner table and ideally the flirting protagonists sit diagonally opposite each other.

A man perceives a woman who approaches him full face or front torso on as potentially threatening and challenging. Unless this is the effect a woman wishes to create, she should approach from a side angle and then slowly move round to face him if she wishes to turn the romantic heat up.

Right: *By touching the sculpture she has moved right into his intimate space zone, and thus has simultaneously brought him into hers. Such close proximity leads to physiological arousal which will be interpreted according to context-specific cues: their eye contact, combined with the tension of their hands, arms and shoulders almost touching, creates an electric atmosphere charged with sexual tension. Yet not a word has been exchanged, and if they so choose, need never be: another love affair that might never happen.*

all. Instead, set up a situation where it becomes possible to offer or receive an open invitation to come closer, or where invasion appears to be in response to an invitation, even if none has been actually offered.

INVITING OTHERS INTO YOUR PERSONAL SPACE

1 Men should initially avoid sitting or standing immediately alongside a woman. The preferred orientation of men and women is different – women feel most at ease if a man approaches them from the front. Once contact is established they feel most

2 Avoid dominance and power plays. Height advantage is often exploited by men to imply power or status. While tall men and high-status men may both be generally rated as being attractive, a bad impression will be created if you imply a need to dominate and control. Thus it is inadvisable to attempt to enter into someone's personal space zone from a position of height. If a man is sitting at a desk – and remember that a large percentage of all romances begin in the workplace – he is unconsciously going to perceive it as attacking or challenging if a woman moves into his space standing up. In the workplace people mark out their territory and guard it jealously. If a woman is on the telephone and a man encroaches on her

territory, for example by putting a briefcase, a cup of coffee or file on her desk or by leaning over the desk or even sitting on it, this will not be conducive to any feelings of attraction.

If, on the other hand, the man indicates with his arms, hands and facial expression that he would like to sit on her desk and permission is readily granted with a nod and a smile, covert or overt feelings of attraction will be in the air. When a woman has the dominant position, power plays are often perceived as particularly disarming by the fragile male ego.

3 In a social setting, if the person whose space you wish to be invited into is sitting down, then you

arousing and attractive. Simultaneously we can give out warm rays of sunlight into which people wish to step. Being in the rays makes them feel good, and in feeling good they are more attracted to the source of the feeling. This human sunlight takes the form of big, sincere and generous smiles, plenty of open gestures, inviting body postures, and a quieter rather than louder voice.

5 Lovers often speak very quietly to each other. It is part of the sexual exchange that takes place within the merged intimate space zones. If we speak clearly but quietly people move closer to us in order to hear us properly. This is a wonderful way of inviting someone to come close. It is also about the

should attempt to lower your eye level to meet theirs. At all times you should remember that the eyes and mouth are central to non-verbal sexual signals. When you are thinking about moving into another person's personal space, you should give consideration as to how best you can align your eyes with theirs.

4 Use open body gestures to create open territory lines into which someone will be attracted to move. This is discussed in much greater detail throughout the book. In principle it means we should create the illusion of being a rewarding door at the end of a triangle-shaped corridor towards which people will be automatically drawn. We want people to feel that the door at the end of the corridor is inviting, tempting, exciting, maybe even a little dangerous,

only good thing going for trying to talk to someone in a bar or nightclub with very loud music – you may have to put your mouth literally to their ear and vice versa to enable any verbal communication at all to take place.

6 If you decide to invade someone's personal space you must override their fear or anger responses by giving them a high dose of positive non-verbal messages. You should move towards them slowly and gently, exchanging brief bursts of eye contact interspersed with lowered eyes, all the time punctuated with a symmetrical smile and small nodding and encouraging movements of the head every five seconds or so. Meanwhile, keep your hands open and expressive and your attitude light and easy rather than intense.

7 When you speak, be positive, flattering, warm and complimentary about them, their tastes, their home – whatever your compliment, they must know your words are really meant for them. Smiles elicit smiles. If you can get someone to open up with a smile their body language and unconscious feelings will soon follow.

8 Once you have connected with someone, the biggest secret of all is to have the courage to back away slightly from them, sending them clear invitations to enter your intimate space zone, and then allowing the other person to advance into your space of their own volition. If they do so, mutual attraction is rapidly building.

Far left: Parties provide excellent settings for observing proxemics. Her arm position acts as a barrier, possibly in response to his side-on approach. Remember, we use our arms and legs to indicate our desired personal space zone. Sensitivity to these signals is vital for successful non-verbal communication.

Left: A man feels most comfortable when a woman approaches him from the side. Once contact is established, men like to communicate with women face to face. Here his arm extends to welcome the woman on his right into his personal space.

Above right: Which couple are more intimate? Your first response is probably to select the pair on the right, but look again. The left-hand couple are mirroring each other's position and their arms and shoulders are virtually touching. The couple on the right, although face-to-face, are less synchronized and less comfortable with their close stance. He is talking quietly, which has caused her to put her face close to his; while this can be a way of drawing someone into the intimate space zone, it may also be unsettling. His posture is stiff and awkward.

MOVING INTO THE INTIMATE ZONE

For someone to invite you into their personal space and, subsequently, their intimate zone, they have to be feeling good about themselves and you. Other people's lives are full of myriad influences over which we have no control. If someone you are very attracted towards is obviously not feeling good, for whatever reason, it will always be a bad time to try to encroach on their intimate space without a specific invitation to do so. It may be that offering someone the physical comfort or the reassurance of an arm, or a shoulder to cry on, is the first intimate contact you establish.

Even simple exchanges between two people can lead one of them to open up. In the letting down of barriers, the mood may change and greater intimacy may be welcomed – for example, by handing someone with their arms tightly crossed a cup of tea, you cause them to lower their defence as they reach out to accept the cup.

The personal space zone is within arm's length; our intimate space zones are variable, depending upon our mood and our relationship with the person with whom we are interacting. Moving into another person's intimate space zone should never be rushed. A change in relative positions induces a rapid and consequential physical change in both people concerned. Remember that to be invited to enter another person's intimate space is a privilege

and a precious gift. It should never be taken for granted and should always be acknowledged very gently, sensitively and sensually.

INVADING SPACE WITH OBJECTS

People often use objects to invade another person's space. Pens, cutlery, wine glasses, cigarettes, candles or whatever can be slid across table tops as if they were chess pieces being sent into battle or ambassadors on a mission to represent our hearts' desire. If you are having a romantic candle-lit dinner and

Above: The synchrony of place settings makes the ever-present space zone boundaries between people almost visible. At the mid-point between the two diners a territorial line is blatantly breached by his hand and knife, which he uses to emphasize his speech. The mirroring of their hand positions, and her provocative fondling of the glass stem (probably unconscious), together with their extended attentive gaze, all suggest that romance is in the air.

Remember that the majority of these non-verbal behaviours take place without our conscious awareness. Commenting aloud on observed unconscious behaviours can be insulting and off-putting. When drawing on knowledge of the many secrets contained within this book, the wiser reader will keep the facts to himself or herself.

Sometimes we leave things behind in people's personal space 'accidentally on purpose': a pair of glasses, a pen on a workmate's desk, an umbrella propped behind a door, a precious piece of clothing; they are all ways of saying that we do not want to leave, and of providing a good excuse for returning another day. This may happen without our being consciously aware of it.

INVADING SPACE WITH OUR BODIES

People invade the personal space of others with various parts of their bodies. Our hands are our most obvious non-verbal communicators. Hands make gestures to represent actual words, to symbolize acts, and to illustrate, emphasize and enliven our verbal conversation. We also use our hands to move into other people's space and we often have ample opportunity to place our hands where they can be touched by another person. From the formal non-threatening handshake to the intimate stroke of a neck or face, the hands are used to indicate interest in another person. The manner in which our hands are employed will indicate the intent that lies behind the gesture. We use our arms and legs too in the personal space dance of love, as you will discover as you train your eyes to observe the details of non-verbal sexual behaviour that occur constantly all around you.

As you move into another person's personal space their body and yours will both respond by sending out numerous non-verbal messages. Some of these will be signals you would rather not be sending and which you may imagine you are controlling. Unfortunately our body mask is never completely foolproof: it leaks. The next chapter examines the secret world of body leakage: the tell-tale signs that talk.

you slide a pen or lighter over the halfway mark of the table and into the other person's space, their reaction will be telling. If they take hold of the object and stroke it, or keep touching it, then they are attracted to you. If they push your object back onto your side of the table, you should back off and accept that romance may not be in the air, or at least take a clear hint that you are rushing things, and they want you to slow down. Men are particularly prone to rush romantic encounters, and would do well to remember that because someone is not immediately attracted to them it does not necessarily mean that they never will be.

OTHER FORMS OF SPACE INVASION

It is sometimes possible to bring two intimate space zones together even across quite a wide physical space. Two people can be arm in arm in their minds even when they are standing 50 feet apart, as, for example, can be witnessed on a dance floor, where strangers at opposite ends of the room may move in perfect synchrony as if they were adjacent to each other, or when someone hugs themselves as if to say, 'This is you in my arms.'

How intimate you are with another person can be indicated dramatically by your body language over some distance. Two people at opposite ends of a train carriage can virtually slow dance with each other without moving from their seats, a delicious conspiracy that excludes the other passengers. We can take people into our intimate space in our imaginations and can indicate our desire with gestures. For example, we can touch a hand against our hearts as if to indicate, 'I would like to hold you to my chest.' Self-touching is discussed in more detail in the chapter on hands (see page 107).

Sometimes pets provide the link that brings people into each other's space. For example, a beautiful and friendly dog on a long lead has been used many a time to reel in an attractive man or woman like a big fish on a hook!

We also use inanimate objects to represent ourselves in other people's space. We give mementoes, letters, flowers and gifts, all of which are symbolic of our actual selves. If a woman knows her postcard is pinned to her target's bedroom wall, then part of her is there in his bedroom with him, even if she has never in fact been to his house. We are in another's intimate space by proxy, as it were. This is why clothes are so intimate; when a woman lends a man her scarf and he wraps it around his neck, then symbolically and perhaps spiritually she is in some way intimately connected with him. The same is true of the time-honoured trick of catching a man's attention by dropping a handkerchief or glove apparently accidentally, but really with the intention of providing him with the chance to be gallant and thereby creating an excuse for making his acquaintance.

Right: The magical moment that precedes a first passionate kiss is charged with tension and excitement. People reserve their intimate space zone for their heart's desire; within its enclave they can touch most parts of each other's bodies and can symbolically become as one being, to the exclusion of the rest of the world.

THE SYMBOLISM OF CARS

For as long as they have existed cars have been used as status symbols. A car serves as an extension of personal space (and sometimes the ego too) but many people don't realize that getting into someone's car is quite an intimate encroachment on the car-owner's space and also a sacrifice of their own space. Cars provide an interesting sexual stage as the physical space boundaries are fixed. For example, in the erotic film The Lover, a scene takes place in the back of a car. The man inches his hand towards the young woman's in minute movements, until at last their fingers touch. As their hands intertwine both of them are looking out of their respective windows, yet from the sensuality of their touch it is obvious that they will inevitably become lovers. Of course, the front seats of cars are where most of the action takes place between courting couples. Driving provides plenty of opportunity for touching 'accidentally on purpose'. The passenger has the advantage over the driver in that he or she can position him or herself to face towards the driver, or lean into the driver's personal space, in a way the driver cannot reciprocate – at least, not without driving dangerously!

CHAPTER TWO

TELL-TALE SIGNS

No matter what we may be saying verbally, or implying with meaningful silences, our bodies carry on a continual dialogue with the outside world. We are very skilled non-verbal communicators principally because, as infants, it takes us such a long time to learn to speak. The pre-speech sounds we make are tremendously expressive, starting right from day one when, newly born, we usually object very vocally to being removed from the womb.

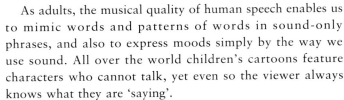

As adults, the musical quality of human speech enables us to mimic words and patterns of words in sound-only phrases, and also to express moods simply by the way we use sound. All over the world children's cartoons feature characters who cannot talk, yet even so the viewer always knows what they are 'saying'.

Non-verbal communication between humans is a complicated business involving the brain in thousands of individual computations per minute as we analyse all the information that we are receiving from our various sense organs. Simultaneously we construct strategies and stimulate signals in response. As you have been reading this text you will probably not have been aware of all the background noises around you, but listen to them for a moment: a clock ticking; a telephone ringing next door; a bird singing; a police siren wailing in the distance; a passing aeroplane; insects buzzing; the heavy deep-sleep breathing of the person in bed next to you. All these sounds are non-verbal communications that we register at some level but do not concentrate our minds upon consciously as the signal does not require action or response.

Selective attention occurs in verbal speech too. For example, when you are at a crowded party where the general volume of chat sounds like a busy swarm of bees, you focus on the conversation taking place immediately in front of you. However, if a

Above: Out of sight, out of mind. Under pressure, feet 'leak' information about our true level of anxiety, tapping and and drawing circles in the air without our realizing it.
Right: Life presents people with numerous situations where non-verbal communications betray private feelings. Twitching fingers, tense shoulders, shallow breathing, biting the lips, nibbling the fingernails, touching the lips – all tell their own story.

30

person three groups away says your name, you immediately hear it above the background noise and may turn to look in that direction.

So our brains are constantly busy, and we can therefore only allocate a percentage of mental energy to monitoring our own non-verbal signals. We tend to concentrate on controlling our faces, as the face is the principal location for interpersonal non-verbal communication.

The face provides the frame for our eyes and mouth – perhaps the two most important individual features in non-verbal sexual signalling – and is in addition capable of expressing myriad moods and

Left: Have a close look at this woman's face. What sort of mood do you think she is in and how are you affected by her expression? You cannot hear her tone of voice, or see any of her body apart from her face, yet you know what she is feeling. The angle of her head, her clenched jaw and taut face muscles, her gritted teeth, her protruding lower lip and jaw as well as her fierce glare with lowered eyebrows and tension around the eyes all send an unequivocal non-verbal message: anger.

feelings. We can be very skilled at controlling our facial expressions (although, as you will read in other chapters, there are still some tell-tale facial movements we cannot control) but we are less skilled at monitoring and containing our body movements and reflexes. When we attempt to control such movements, or even fool ourselves that we are exerting such control, our body still relentlessly continues to send out its non-verbal messages. These ticks and twitches that talk are referred to by psychologists as the 'non-verbal leakage' of information. Leakage is a good word, as the plumbing parallel is appropriate: you may believe that the welding on the joint of a pipe is utterly sound, yet under pressure it starts to leak. Research suggests

that we are especially prone to leakage at the periphery of our bodies – our hands, fingers and feet. This is why people being interviewed for high-pressure jobs are often seated in a lonely chair in the middle of a room with no desk to hide behind, enabling the interviewers to get the 'whole picture'. The leakage seems to act like a pressure-release safety valve which is difficult to control. If we stop our fingers drumming, our feet start tapping instead; if we concentrate on keeping our feet still, then perhaps a shoulder or elbow will twitch. Actors and mime artists spend hundreds of hours training themselves to control the whole picture, so it is not surprising that the rest of us find it so difficult.

Twitches and ticks relate to various other patterns of non-verbal sexual communication that will be referred to throughout the book and are explained below. They should be remarked upon in the context of the situation and cross-referenced to other simultaneously occuring non-verbal signals. The following section introduces some of the principle areas of knowledge you will need to acquire in order to develop your interpretive skills.

KEY CONCEPTS OF NON-VERBAL SEXUAL SIGNALS

The following descriptive phrases refer to sex-related communications phenomena that occur in most encounters between and women.

Context
Whenever you are studying non-verbal sexual signals you must take the context in which the transactions are taking place into account. This may seem obvious but it's surprising how many people are unaware of sending inappropriate signals in many settings. For example, the boundaries between business and social transactions are clearly

defined by cultural convention yet many men and women are careless in observing the unwritten conventions for business, using non-verbal sexual signals to 'persuade' without apparently anticipating the predictable and sometimes embarrassing responses such flirtations can evoke.

Environmental factors, particularly temperature, can strongly affect our body language – for example, we tend to fold our arms and hug ourselves in the cold. It may simply be that someone you are interested in who has adopted an apparently defensive arm-crossed stance may simply be freezing to death! At formal events, where people are required to adopt stiff postures, relaxed interpersonal communication will be difficult. Tight or very elaborate clothes also restrict natural body movement.

Pointing

When we are attracted to someone we will often point at them – not obviously, with a finger, but quietly and seductively, with our eyes, our hands and arms, our legs, feet and toes. It is as if we want to unconsciously indicate our sexual interest in someone by pointing at them to select them from a crowd. This also seems to serve as an unconscious indicator to make our intentions clear to others present.

We also point with our hands at our own best sexual assets, and also at the parts of our body most significant for a particular non-verbal communication, for example our eyes. Being alert to pointing empowers you to analyse what is happening between people, and learning how to point at the right parts of you at the right time will give you a significant non-verbal advantage over those who do not know this secret!

Peek-a-boo

This is a very simple game that we all play as infants and continue to play in a variety of forms in our adult lives, particularly during the process of

seduction. It is a source of disproportionate pleasure and is so important in our lives that you will find a whole chapter (Chapter 6) devoted to it. In this chapter you will discover that not only do we play peek-a-boo with our eyes, we also employ various bits of our bodies in this delicous game. We flash our flesh at each other through gaps and tears in our clothes, tapping into those early, intensely joyful memories of peek-a-boo when it was one of the few games we were able to play. It is even possible for an actor to play peek-a-boo with just his eyes with members of the audience sitting in the front seats of a theatre.

Right: Never judge a book by its cover: non-verbal communication can be ambiguous. Most people's judgements of others' thoughts and feelings is based on insufficient information. Clarification gained by checking for additional body signals always triumphs over assumption. The girl here appears timid, even fearful, but she may be sad. She may even be angry: some people find showing certain feelings very difficult. More information is required to be sure of reaching the correct interpretation.

Blocking

As you have already learnt, our sexual body language is dramatically affected by the distances between us and other people, and the degree to which our personal body space is invaded. The study of personal space – proxemics – gives us access to all sorts of fascinating insights and secrets about the way we can create the space most conducive to successful seduction. A common mistake, made especially by men, is to block a woman into a corner or up against a bar so as to stifle her or make her feel trapped. The art of blocking is to establish boundaries around you and the person whom you are attempting to seduce in such a way as to create a private and safe haven, not a claustrophobic cell. More established lovers do this very obviously with their arms interlocking, or with coats drawn up to form a small tent within which to kiss and cuddle, or even just with their intense mutual gaze from which the rest of the world feels excluded, and within which the lovers are oblivious, entranced by each other's eyes.

We block successfully by using our bodies as shields to protect the object of our desire and to rebuff any potential predators or rival suitors. This

Above: Our faces are capable of hundreds of different expressions, thanks to the complex muscle structures beneath the skin. The expression of peekaboo is almost audible.

Left: A relaxed, balanced expression indicates openness and sincerity. When a smile is genuine the whole face seems to smile.

Right: Surprise is indicated by the wide eyes, raised eyebrows and open mouth. The sparkling eyes and lack of mouth distortion differentiate this look from that of terror.

Below right: Humans are brilliant mimics of facial expressions. If you copy this face you will probably feel sad.

is particularly important at parties or in informal social meeting places, where men particularly are apt to be very competitive and ambitious in their pursuit of female company. This is not to say that woman are uncompetitive; they just tend to use a less aggressive style.

Once we have established a relatively intimate interaction with another individual, we need to mark out our territory in such a way as to assert our power while simultaneously excluding others yet including our interactant in comfort. Blocking is also a useful skill for sending 'I'm not interested' messages without having the embarrassment of needing to spell it out in words. By building a wall with non-verbal blocks around us we can protect ourselves, comfort ourselves and warn others off; our arms, legs, shoulders and body position can all be employed as a means of saying 'no thanks'. It is useful to be able to do this for ourselves, and also to recognize such signals in others – it may save egos from being too dented.

POSTURAL ECHOING AND MIRRORING

When we are attracted to someone else it is usually for one of two principal reasons: either we perceive a similarity between us and them or we anticipate a complementarity. The similarity theory suggests that the person we are most attracted to will be very like us in many respects: looks, height, personality, background, taste in music, star sign, religion, you name it. The greater the number of shared understandings courting couples identify the more they imagine sharing their space and building a long-term relationship together. Research into successful long-term relationships supports this view. As the social commentator Kathy Chubb put it, 'similarity breeds content'. At its narcissistic extreme, we unconsciously seek out the opposite sex version of ourselves. The complementary theory suggests that we seek a partner who has the qualities we miss in ourselves. In forming a bond with someone who complements us we become 'complete'. This can lead us to form dependent relationships that may put untenable pressure on one or both parties.

The ideal is perhaps a combination of these two contrasting positions – an integration of 'sameness' and 'differentness' that is a central feature of the human condition: the struggle for contentment in the face of endless paradox. However, during the early stages of a romantic encounter, we do automatically highlight the qualities of sameness. This expresses itself in two forms: the first is with postural echoes and the second is in mirroring behaviour.

Posture echo is when one person takes up a particular body posture and the other follows them,

moving to adopt a similar or even identical posture between five and 50 seconds later. If you notice that someone has echoed your posture you can be sure that they are comfortable in your company and probably attracted to you too. You can test how interested they are in being 'like' you by deliberately changing your body position and noting if they follow the change. The more they follow you the more interested they are.

You do not have to initiate the postural changes – you can follow the other person's movements.

This will have the effect of sending them a strong signal of sexual interest. However, if they keep changing positions as soon as you follow them, they may be sending you an unconscious 'not interested' message, or they may be saying, 'You're going too fast, slow it down a bit, please.' In any case, back off both physically and non-verbally. Turn down the heat a bit.

The real art is to echo the other person's posture without copying them exactly. It is possible to suggest the same stance without mimicking it exactly. The effect is to capture the spirit of the position of the other person. By doing this you are moving towards mirroring.

As you become attracted to someone you begin to tune into their wavelength and, if the feelings are mutual, they tune into yours. Some couples report that after only a short time together they seem to be able to think and move in synchrony. It is as if they have become one person, reaching for their drinks or folding their arms simultaneously, leaning forwards or back like choreographed dancers. You become each other's reflection moving in unison, showing each other non-verbally that you are bonding. This has the effect of both individuals feeling potent, affirmed, recognized, wanted, attractive, warm and desirable, and will make the experience feel more sincere, more real, more meaningful.

Research has shown that people who are very much in love, or close friends who have known each other a long time, automatically develop this ability to tune in to the smallest movement. We mirror tiny facial twitches; nods and blinks; lip tremors, tone and accent of voice, speed of speech; tiny head nods or shakes; small shoulder shrugs; hand gestures and non-verbal vocal sounds, like 'mmmmhh' and 'ooooh'. We can find ourselves not only reaching for a drink in synchrony with our friend or lover but making the same lip smacking and breathy sounds in appreciation of the contents of the glass. Mirroring even occurs at a physiological level – the rate and depth of breathing may be

synchronized, metabolic rate and blood pressure may become similar. More obviously, we use similar hand gestures, take up matching body torso postures, and tilt our heads to the same angle, helping to keep our eyes aligned.

Mirroring takes two main forms: if your partner has their right elbow on a table at which you are sitting face to face you can either put your left elbow on the table to match your partner's right elbow (full mirroring) or you can put your right elbow on the table (half mirroring). Which option you choose will depend on the context of your encounter. When sitting opposite each other eating a meal a couple can half mirror by lifting forks to

Above: The position of his arm on the bar explains the situation without any need for words; he is using it like a fortress wall, symbolizing a shield to protect the woman who is object of his desire while simultaneously rebuffing a rival suitor.

Left: Two women sitting at a bar send profoundly different non-verbal messages to interested observers: the one on the left shows total blocking compared with being open to, and probably appreciative of, a potential approach. She demonstrates an upright yet relaxed and confident posture, with unfolded arms, the face and torso turned towards the room, and eyes ready to connect with the glances of others. She is inviting approach, in contrast to the cold and closed-off signals of the other woman.

Right: This couple are fully mirroring each other's position and movements, indicating that a strong mutual attraction is present and a consequent desire for synchrony as a prelude to further intimacy.

mouths in synchrony, both using the left hand. If they are standing side by side at a bar it is easier and a more powerful non-verbal sexual signal to do a full mirror movement.

PUTTING IT INTO PRACTICE

How can you use mirroring to your own advantage early on? The first rule is: don't play 'copy cat' – you will be sussed quickly by the other person. Secondly, if the other person is genuinely interested, some mirroring will already be happening. The art is to speed up the process by deliberately increasing the degree of echo and mirroring behaviour. This has the effect of exaggerating the positive feelings of attraction that may already be developing. Sometimes you may discover yourself mirroring someone to whom you were not sure of feeling attracted. An increased sense of self-awareness is one of the most valuable skills you can develop when you are learning to enhance your non-verbal communication skills. If you can manage to ignore all the different thoughts that are whirling around in your head and focus your concentration instead on what your own body language is telling you, you will find yourself increasingly attracted towards people who are also attracted to you.

Remember, the way to become expert in all these different skills is through application and practice. The purpose of this book is to accomplish a movement of non-verbal translation from an unconscious to a conscious level. Once you become conscious of your own and other people's pointing, blocking, context, posture echo and mirroring, new worlds of communication open up for you. With practice anyone can become a far more accurate interpreter of what other people are thinking and feeling.

Look at the world around you: watch the television with the sound turned down. Try studying your favourite actors and analyse their body language. What is there about it that you like so much? What are their most sensuous movements?

Left: Early in their encounter both the man and the woman automatically cover their sexual body areas but they are interested in continuing their dialogue. They hold each other's eye gaze and unconsciously begin to mirror the other's postures: each has one leg in the water and their arms are in strikingly similar poses.

Above: Smiling, he moves closer, turning his torso towards her, pointing at her with both knees and left arm and leaning his upper body and head into her personal space. She maintains a relatively cautious position but her raised left shoulder and relaxed smile indicate that she feels some attraction for him, though as yet she may not be conscious of it.

Right: Some time later the woman has rearranged her body position into a much more relaxed and accepting stance. Her head leaning towards the man, her obvious acceptance of his close proximity and and the way in which her knees are drawn up, sending an unconscious sexual signal by mimicking breasts, all suggest that strong mutual attraction exists between them and that a romantic interlude may well ensue as a result of their meeting.

Can you replicate them? If you have a video player, watch your favourite clips in slow motion or freeze them frame by frame. This is the technique many psychologists have used in their pioneering research and you can do it for yourself at home.

If you have a video camcorder, make films at parties or at public places like railway stations or airports, where there are hundreds of romantic greetings and farewells every day. If you are feeling really brave you can ask a friend to video you at a party. You will be self-conscious to start with but after a time you will forget the camera is on you. Later, analyse your own body language when you are interacting with members of the opposite sex, and theirs too. You will very soon be able to identify various elements of the secret non-verbal language about which you have been reading.

The world is your very own private university, full of information for you to learn; the players in this wonderful game are all around you. So let us proceed with a look at the first impressions you make. As you will see, first impressions are vitally important in the mating game. If you are like most people, you may often have made a mess of the first few minutes and as a result missed many potential romantic liaisons. With care, you can establish a romantic, attraction-filled episode from the first moment you meet someone.

CHAPTER THREE

LOVE AT FIRST SIGHT

You walk into a crowded party thronged with people dancing, drinking and chatting. As you enter the room one or two people will notice you. How long they look at you and the major decisions they make about you will depend almost entirely on the non-verbal signals you display. Unbelievable as it may seem, we form our main impressions about people within the first two minutes of interacting with them – which can mean simply watching them across a room for a couple of minutes after they arrive. Worse, we are often reluctant to let go of our initial assumptions about

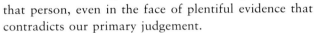

that person, even in the face of plentiful evidence that contradicts our primary judgement.

'Never judge a book by its cover' is a worthy saying, yet much of the time we ignore it. We live in a world where the clothes, haircut and jewellery we wear and the way we carry our bodies are all judged instantly by everyone we meet.

Through rapid mental gymnastics we analyse the visual information we receive about other people. We cross-reference their various visual clues with thousands of previously memorized 'cards' in our visual database and produce a category for them to be slotted into, often based upon ridiculous stereotypes or prejudices we came across as children and have never rid ourselves of. We make outrageous snap judgements about people's personalities, class, wealth, occupations, success, good or bad qualities and even sexual skills, basing those judgements on the very minimum of information.

By making assumptions, positive or negative, your brain may be doing you and them no favours whatsoever. But do not be too hard on yourself: everyone does it! So, given the fact that we do stereotype people on the basis of their looks, how can we use this fact to our advantage? The answer is twofold.

Above and right: *What is your first impression of the couple holding hands in the photograph on the right? Do you see two men, a man and a woman or two women? Things are not always as they first appear to be. However, the very moment we see other people we automatically make assumptions about them in order to be able to predict and control their behaviour towards us.*

THE POWER OF CLOTHES

First, we should always keep in mind that the clothes we wear make a loud non-verbal statement about who we are, what we stand for, how much we care about our appearance and fashion trends, and how interested we are in displaying our sexuality. Once again we are faced with a dilemma: dressing very provocatively, especially in the case of women, is likely to attract a great deal of sexual attention. The more overtly sexual clothing is, the more members of the opposite gender will be aroused, but arousal is not the same as attraction. Arousal might be the effect you are after, but consider the likely detrimental side-effects. What will your clothes say to her or him about you as a potential long-term boyfriend or girlfriend? What will people of the same sex think of you? Will they feel threatened by your flaunted sexuality? Will you be labelled unflatteringly? Will people take you for a teaser? Or will they be right to assume that you are into power games and control?

Everything about your clothes carries a non-verbal message, and many clothes bear verbal messages as well: designer labels and T-shirt slogans, for example, make an impression. Even the colours, the cut and the texture of clothes affect the way we are perceived by others.

The colours of our clothes in particular speak volumes. The 'hot' colours, especially scarlet, are all linked with sexuality. Bright red actually makes us physically aroused – breathing and heart rates rise in the presence of strong red colours. We literally warm up in a fashion similar to that when we are becoming sexually turned on. The 'red rag' effect is a myth when it comes to bulls, but not with humans. A red dress is particularly sexual and the wearer should expect to attract a swarm of over-excited admirers. In a recent experiment, college students were shown photographs of the same woman dressed soberly or provocatively in a sexually revealing outfit. In the latter image, she was consistently judged by both men and women to be more sexually active, flirtatious, willing to use her sexuality for personal advantage and more likely to be unfaithful. This is clearly ridiculous, yet it shows that when we have no other information upon which to make sound assessments, our imaginations automatically run wild and create judgements about people that are based on nothing more than speculation.

The red coats worn by various armies over several centuries, now redundant save for ceremonial uniforms and formal 'mess' kits, are dramatically sexy – as any female tourist will tell you as she admires guardsmen on sentry duty outside St James's Palace in London! In the last few years men in the West have started to wear much brighter colours, though in most work settings they are still restricted to traditional attire of sober-coloured suits.

Other colours do carry significant non-verbal messages. Consider the effects of wearing bright white from head to toe, for example, or of dressing in black. Ask yourself how the colours make you feel, and also what effect they might have on someone you want to attract.

Once in a relationship you may choose to dress for your partner, but initially you should dress for yourself. Wear clothes that make you feel good, enhance your best features and send a message that concords with the image you want to project on any particular occasion.

Our imaginations play a central role in the early formation of relationships. One of the greatest 'turn ons' is imagining the parts of another person's body that we cannot see. Clothes that hint at what lies below the folds of material are much more exciting than show-it-all displays in short skirts or shirts unbuttoned to the waist. A long skirt with a discreet split that occasionally reveals a flash of leg is infinitely more alluring to a man. In the same way, men's clothes that suggest a fine body are usually sexier to women than skin-tight T-shirts and spray-on jeans.

These are generalizations, however: many individual preferences exist, some common, some less common, others bizarre. You will be aware of

Above: Every part of our attire speaks volumes about our personality, status, age and perhaps even our occupation. Wherever we go people will assess us visually just as we assess others.

Left: This woman's stance is both overtly sexual and quite aggressive; her figure-hugging, brightly coloured top draws attention to her breasts, which she displays brazenly. Overtly sexual clothes are often judged as being surprisingly unsexy by both women and men.

Right: Contrast the effect on your perception of this woman by glancing back and forth between the photograph on the left and this one on the right. The dull-coloured jacket, the absence of challenging eye contact and the hiding of the thighs give a completely different impression. Pop and film stars wishing to go about their daily business unnoticed simply dress down.

Above: Psychologists study identical twins in order to identify the differences in the way humans are affected by the environment and by genetics. Many twins have markedly different personalities. One glance at these twins enables us to spot personality clues. Or does it? Can you really judge which sister is the more confident, outgoing, successful, relaxed or approachable?

your own inclinations, such as, 'I only go out with tall men', 'I only date blondes', 'I like my men hairy', 'I love big girls, never looked at a skinny woman in my life', and so on. The trouble with such thoughts is that they limit our choice. We box ourselves in by viewing potential sexual partners with blinkered vision. While making a judgement based on a stereotypical viewpoint is a natural human response, by sticking to your first impression you are severely restricting your field. Rather, you should use the automatic response as a starting point from which you can depart further and further the more you find out about a person.

In Western society we regard people's work as a significant indicator of status and personality, and we attach assumed desirability levels to careers in a hierarchical fashion. Until recently, our society was virtually uniformed. People identified their membership of particular social groups and occupations by wearing specific sets of clothes. We still assume that it is possible to guess a person's job just by judging their attire. What you wear will create an immediate impression on others and on the way you feel about yourself, so take time to re-examine your clothes and ask yourself what signals you might be sending.

Prior to the exchange of verbal information, there will be many other non-verbal clues to the status and personality of the person to whom you are attracted. Women and men alike pick up on these clues, although women are better at this particular skill than men. Non-verbal indicators include wedding rings, signet rings, diamond rings, other jewellery, watches and shoes. The latter say a great deal about us because they are at the periphery of our bodies, but they often receive the least care. How high or low are the heels? How clean are the shoes? How well made? How fashionable or traditional? Good-quality, well-made shoes are always a sign of high status, and the possession of high status increases our sexual attraction.

CONFIDENCE, POWER AND STATUS

Whether we like it or not, status is a reliable pre-dictor of sexual attraction. This is why first impressions are so important – especially as we tend to distort any subsequent information, verbal or non-verbal, that we receive about a person to fit our initial impression. If we rate someone as being highly attractive, sexy and desirable the moment we see them we will actively discriminate in their favour.

Apart from the obvious symbols of status such as clothing and accessories, an impres-sion of power can be created by a combina-tion of the way we use our eyes, how com-fortable we look in our bodies, how relaxed our faces appear and the degree to which our muscle tone looks firm and well-shaped. These are all things over which you have the power of change and choice.

Our body language reflects the way we feel about ourselves. The higher our self-esteem, the more comfortable we look in our bodies and the more attractive we become. Low self-esteem is a principal cause of anxi-ety and social discomfort. Feeling confident allows us to take more risks and protects us from disappointment if a romantic approach fails. Take a sheet of paper and make a list of all the things you like about yourself. This is not an incitement to be big-headed; it is to help you realize that you have a much greater chance of other people liking or lov-ing you if you are conscious of liking or even loving yourself. The more you like yourself, the more you will wear your body around you in comfort. The more comfortable you look, the more attractive you will be to oth-ers. When we feel good about ourselves we tend to hold ourselves upright – not in a stiff or stretched fashion, but balanced and tall. Actual height does not matter (although for some reason taller men are rated as being more attractive), it is presence that counts. The authority with which you command your own body directly affects the way you

Below: A relaxed yet upright, friendly demeanour suggests an established sense of self-worth. Inner confidence is reflected in posture, choice of clothes, hairstyle and, especially, in facial expression. A broad grin gives us the immediate impression that this is a cheerful person, and this in turn makes him more attractive. In fact he was photographed flirting with a woman in the adjacent telephone booth.

are perceived by others. Whenever you can, keep both feet flat on the ground: this has the effect of calming you and controlling your balance, which creates a better impression on others and makes you feel more confident too.

SHAKING HANDS

A handshake says so much about us: our hands animate our spoken words but also speak their own language. Look at your own hands for a minute. What do they say about you? How big are they? What shape are they? How rough or soft is the skin of your palms? How fleshy are your pads?

What temperature are they? Is one hand hotter than the other? Are they damp, and are you aware of how this changes depending on your state of emotional arousal?

Look at your nails. Are they clean and cut into a clear shape or are they dirty (a major turn-off, especially for women)? Do you bite your nails? If you do, have a good look at your chewed stubs and ask yourself how they might make someone else feel in a potentially romantic situation?

When you greet someone, do you shake hands with confidence or doubt? One does not need to squeeze the life out of another person's hand. It is hardly going to make a woman feel attracted to a man if he hurts her in his enthusiasm to impress

LOVE AT FIRST SIGHT

Below: Look at the people in this bus queue. What judgements do you make about their personalities, status, attractiveness, careers, ages, backgrounds? Your assumptions will reflect prejudices and stereotypes that you may often project onto strangers. Remember to avoid being blinkered in your judgements of other people while at the same time being sensitive to the first impressions you are making yourself. The picture shows a model, a literary editor, a history of art student, a book designer, an actor and a psychotherapist, but can you guess who is who? (The answer is that they are in the same order as this list, but from right to left.)

his status upon her. Nor will it impress a man of a woman's status if she shakes hands so limply it feels as if her arm were dead.

Numerous experiments have been carried out by psychologists into the effects of various styles of handshake. By far the most favourable first impression made by both men and women was when the handshake lasted five seconds and was firm without being uncomfortable. Furthermore, a dry palm makes a better impression as a sweaty palm may signify nervousness. This, combined with assured eye contact, a slight smile towards the middle of the handshake moving to a wider smile at the last stage of the handshake and a small tilt of the head to one side, forms the ultimate positive impression. A handshake can have a lasting effect on the impression we make on others and the degree to which they find us attractive.

Research shows that people of high status tend to shake hands with their palms facing downwards. This may unconsciously increase status in the eyes of the other person, but may also warn them that this person likes to dominate their partner. People less concerned with power tend to offer a hand in which the thumb is on top. However, do remember that a weak or palm-up handshake does not automatically mean the person is submitting to your dominance; cultural differences exist and some people's careers require them to guard their hands with protective care.

The hands can be used to convey many non-verbal signals of sexual desire too, and these are discussed in detail in Chapter 9.

Whether arriving at a party, entering a room for a job interview or meeting a blind date, we only have two minutes to create a first impression. Central to our success in achieving the maximum positive effect is understanding the secrets of attraction. Chapter 4 examines the key issues of interpersonal attraction by revealing the elements that affect how we judge others and ourselves as being romantically appealing.

CHAPTER FOUR

ATTRACTION
AND AESTHETICS

The question of what we find attractive in others and what we can do to enhance our own best assets is a major preoccupation during at least some part of our lives. Sadly, the ideal lovers of sexual fantasies are usually completely unrealistic because our relationship to them is over-simplistic, lacking intimacy, bonding or emotional commitment. A principal pleasure in imagining seducing or being seduced by your fantasy lover is his or her unavailablity in real life. Understanding the secrets of attraction will enable you to relate to others in a more fulfilling way.

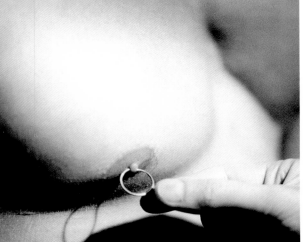

THE HEAT OF THE CHASE

The male love of The Chase is universal, though this may be changing as we approach the 21st century. It seems that women are finally breaking out of the passive role within the early rituals of non-verbal sexual seduction. Traditionally, it would appear that men have always been expected to make the first move, whether hunting for food to feed potential offspring, fighting rivals for the prize of a maiden's hand, or wooing with endless written, sung or spoken declarations of romantic love, accompanied by numerous presents ranging from single handpicked flowers to trunkloads of treasure.

Has all this been a foolish male conspiracy to keep womankind passive, weak and vulnerable? Or is the reality that women have always had to be very choosy about selecting their mate as, once committed, the long-term consequences of child-rearing are enormous. The latter point has some truth, the former is less convincing. Women are rarely truly 'passive' when they are being persuaded by potential lovers. On the contrary, they often control men like mere puppets on strings, manoeuvring

Above: Would you want your nipple pierced? Such are the vagaries of attraction – what revolts some delights others. Variety is the spice of life and, perhaps, of love.
Right: Some women like to dominate their lover, while a minority of men are sexually fixated on particular parts of the body. While toe-sucking might not be to everyone's taste, some people find this pastime an essential precursor to sexual arousal.

the pace and intensity of their various suitors' advances like a general moves armies about a map. It is usually the women who, with a subtle variety of non-verbal signals combined with higher visual accuracy and a generally elevated intuition, initiate the chase. An invitation to this ritual a man cannot resist. How can he, when one glance across a room can set a heart aflame?

Traditionally, the woman has thrown down the gauntlet and if the man has had his eyes open wide enough to spot it he has been expected to pick it up and start running. This 'chase' phenomenon may link with the irresistibility of peek-a-boo; it is certainly a similar dynamic process, and also has an element of voyeuristic pleasure to it too. The feminine opening gambit is like being shown a brief glimpse of treasure without the requisite map to aid in its discovery.

However, it seems things are changing. In North America especially, it is now quite common for a woman to make the first overt move, to initiate conversation, even to swagger and strut when in the presence of a man she finds attractive, and rather than 'follow' she takes the physical lead in proceeding up the step-by-step ladder of non-verbal behaviours that lead to a full sexual commitment. Most cultures, though, still expect the man to apparently take the initiative while in reality following her subtle commands. Perhaps an ideal will be reached when each male and female takes an equal responsibility and active engagement in advancing into a sexual relationship.

In accepting equality most of us still have a long way to go. The ideal, however, should be kept in the forefront of the mind. It spares us the intense emotional pain of unrequited love and the endless, almost compulsive pursuit of someone who just does not fancy us or love us in the same way.

One fallacious contention of many writers is that endless persistence, particularly by men, will eventually persuade a person of the correctness of the suitor's point of view; that is to say, it is possible to talk someone into liking you, going to bed with you or loving you. This kind of thinking is potentially dangerous for both parties concerned because if a relationship of some sort does result

the more reluctant partner will not feel easy in that relationship. All too often people end up with an unsuitable partner despite their intuitive reading of their own or their partner's body language. Warning thoughts such as, 'You really don't fancy this person, so why are you letting them kiss you?' breed not affection but self-revulsion. Listen to these warnings and act upon them. Sometimes your reasoning head will tell you one thing and your feeling heart will suggest another. (Men tend to be more thinking and women more feeling.) If you normally act upon one source of internal information, stop a while to ask yourself about the feelings or thoughts generated by the other source.

TUNE IN

Of course people do grow to love people over time, while 'love at first sight' is sometimes lost. Nothing in life is concrete; we change in our tastes all the time. What and who we find attractive is highly fluid – we are all friends with at least one

Above right: If all men had heroic Greek figures would they be so highly prized? Men are prone to hypocrisy when it comes to body shape. They expect women to be unnaturally thin or shapely, yet often leave their own bodies flabby and untended. The extremes of obsessive body building or total neglect of fitness are equally unattractive. Being physically active and fit makes people feel healthy and generally better about themselves, and they therefore feel and appear more attractive.

Right: Western culture's obsession with the androgynous body shape apparently flies in the face of nature's design: women have more body fat and less muscle mass than men. The very antithesis of a sexually mature woman being heralded as physically alluring can perhaps only be explained by the assumed desirability of youth above all else.

Continually reminding yourself that you are able to change your mind about other people and what attracts you to them is a way of escaping the limitations in life that we all too often construct around us. As you enhance your love of variety and your love affair with life, so your love of yourself will grow. By trying to be optimistic and positive you can obtain a much greater level of contentment in your life, and develop an understanding that a wider scope of what is attractive to you in other people will greatly enhance the likelihood of your meeting someone to whom you are very attracted and who is attracted to you.

We all have expectations of people's characters and personalities and we base these on physical appearance. Research shows these expectations are usually inaccurate. We are continually bombarded with mass-media-conceived images of what is attractive, yet most of us fail to match these images. Nevertheless, as we shall see, there are some rational explanations for what we find attractive in others.

person whom we did not like when we first met them. In the same way that first impressions about people can be completely wrong, our feelings of attraction are sometimes unreliable.

The surer you are of your own likes and dislikes the more attractive you are to others, because self-confidence is usually rated as being attractive. But remember that being a good listener, together with showing sensitivity to the feelings of those around you, can be equally attractive.

Your aesthetic intuition counts for a lot. Be careful how much you let your intrusive intellect muscle in on territory best dominated by your gut feelings. Tune in to your own body language as you come close to someone of the opposite sex.

Practising self-analysis will heighten your ability to read the non-verbal signals of others. If you find yourself in the common bind of saying one thing and thinking or doing another, examine your own non-verbal messages and change your spoken words accordingly. The integration of thoughts and feelings is a difficult goal worth striving for.

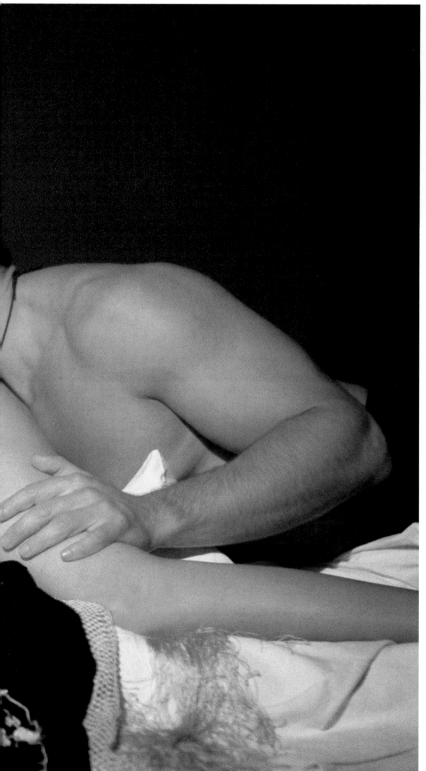

Above and left: Throughout history humans have attempted to solve the secrets of attraction, trying to acquire knowledge that would increase their success in love. In our modern age, when long-term relationships so often seem statistically doomed to failure, there is a nostalgia for romance and a yearning for long-lasting love. In the early stages of courting, couples spend extended periods of time gazing into each other's eyes and exploring and touching every part of each other's bodies. These central ingredients of attachment that fire excitement and fulfilment are essential, and should be repeatedly worked at so that after the initial flush of enthusiasm has passed ongoing mutual attraction can be maintained, enhanced with such qualities as honesty, sensitivity, gentleness, honour, loyalty and fidelity.

GENDER SIGNALS

There are certain key physical differences between men and women that enable us to differentiate between the sexes in the space of an instant. No matter what race the individual may belong to, it is these traits or 'gender signals' that stand out. While the chart below is exemplary rather than comprehensive, it is a true example of sexual dimorphism. It is worth noting here that obsession with the average, or burdening yourself with a fetish for the conventional, may be unhealthy and certainly unhelpful in the quest for a partner.

On this quest, exceptions to the middle rule abound, fortunately loosening limitations. This encourages happiness and increases chances for connubial success. For example, experiments have shown that men who are bald or balding are less sexually attractive, yet there are women who think bald men are by far the earth's sexiest creatures.

To generalize about features that are or are not attractive is to do yourself and everyone around you an enormous disservice. It is simply not the case that all red-headed people are fiery tempered, or that all blondes are less intelligent or are sexually more skilled, or that large-breasted women are more sexually aware or active, or that people who wear glasses are more intelligent.

WOMEN	MEN	WOMEN	MEN
A space and gentle mound at the apex of the legs	A bulge at the apex of the legs	Muscle less massive	Muscle more massive
Hips wider in relation to the waist	Hips narrower in relation to the waist	Shorter stature	Taller stature
Narrower waist and shoulders	Wider waist and shoulders	Less hair on body and face	Hairier
Elbows closer to the body	Elbows away from the body	Hardly discernible Adam's apple	Prominent Adam's apple
Proportionately more fat and with a different distribution	Proportionately less fat and with a different distribution	Softer, smoother skin	Skin less smooth, less soft
Buttocks protruding more	Buttocks protruding less	Higher pitched voice	Lower pitched voice
Greater buttock movement when walking	Less buttock movement when walking	Age-related baldness rare	Age-related baldness common
Pronounced breasts	Undeveloped breasts	Fleshier lips	Less fleshy lips
Smaller skeletal frame (hands and feet especially)	Larger skeletal frame	Less bushy eyebrows	Bushier eyebrows
		More sensitive skin	Less sensitive skin
		Shoulders and knees rounded	Shoulders and knees less rounded

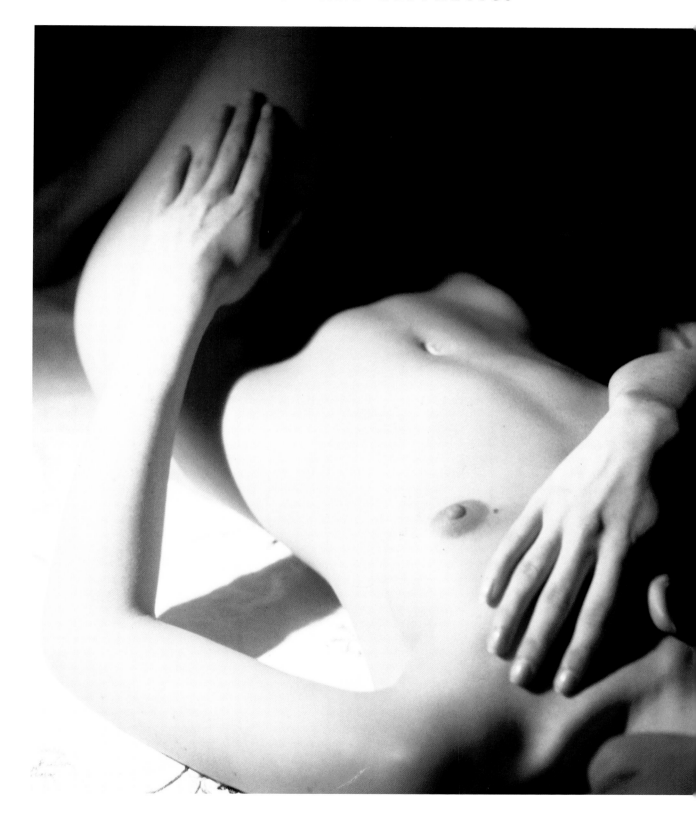

Top left: A man sits opposite his partner discussing why he has been out of contact with her for several days. Before reading on, examine each of the images and ask yourself which signals you think suggest dishonesty. Open palms, direct eye contact and a sincere symmetrical smile indicate that the truth is being told.

Top right: The shrug of the shoulders, combined with a look of exasperation at not being believed and the turning in of the fingers, suggest that he may be lying.

Bottom left and right: His open left palm is vulnerable and appealing, as is his disarming smile, yet he is rubbing his face. Perhaps he is not telling the whole truth.

Many of the individual non-verbal sexual signals that we shall go on to identify will make more sense in the context of these principal gender signals. No matter how sophisticated and cultivated we think we are, we continue to function at a primitive level. This behaviour is by no means restricted to the subconscious.

The principal needs that motivate us are food, drink, sleep and sex. We spend a third of our lives asleep and a good deal of our waking lives working in order to earn money so as to nourish ourselves and create a life in which we are most likely to enjoy regular sex. We spend a lot of time thinking about food and drink – its purchase, its aethetics, its preparation, its rituals, its implications – worrying about sleep if we're not getting sufficient and thinking about sex.

Sex is a principal source of pleasure in our lives, but it is also the subject of considerable misunderstanding and anxiety. The joys of sex are easily lost in the face of emotional upset, stress or self-doubt. Many people torment themselves with anxiety about physical appearance, finding numerous imperfections in themselves or others. The critical

voice in our heads that always judges others, picking on their clothes, hair, height, shape, voice and so on does nothing but harm and tends to leave us bitter and resentful. This in turn lowers our self-esteem, though we hide behind a veneer of arrogance, and renders us less attractive to others while simultaneously making us over-critical of potential lovers. Everybody loses in the end.

Ask yourself who you find attractive and why. Are you a slave to fashion advertising? Do you give people marks out of ten for sex appeal in your head as you walk through a crowd? Do you have a stereotypical view of beauty?

How we perceive a person's exterior often changes dramatically as we start to get a better idea of their character. Over time the discrepancy between our perception of the exterior and interior diminishes and we can come to see people as they really are. Thus a person with a beautiful appearance can begin to seem ugly, and someone very plain-looking can become ravishing.

Our sexual communication skills serve us best after we confront the truth of who we are inside, integrating this into how we present ourselves to the world. The greater the congruence between inner and outer self, the more 'real' our sexual relationships will be.

Meaningful attraction is a reflection of our inner sense of self, but initial external attraction is based on a combination of highlighted gender signals and media-contrived fashions and fads: big bust vs small bust; short hair vs long hair; flares vs tubes; heavy make-up vs the natural look; sun tan vs white skin, etc. How do we integrate these apparently incompatible positions? The answer is to be found through compromise. We must work on enhancing both our sense of self internally and the image that we present to the world. This book is concerned with the messages we convey non-verbally. Inner self-esteem grows as we enhance the way we look. Wearing something we like cheers us up. The clothes we wear, our hair style, the degree of care we spend in cleaning and grooming ourselves can all contribute to the way in which we view ourselves.

SIGNALS OF DECEPTION

People often ask psychologists if they can read what people are thinking just by observing their body language and, in particular, whether they can tell if someone is lying.

We are usually brought up to think that lying is bad. Most of us are encouraged to develop a keen sense of right and wrong and to feel guilty if we avoid telling the truth. As a result, as with any strong emotion, conflicts that occur inside us tend to leak out, showing themselves in our non-verbal behaviour. The extent to which this leakage shows itself when we lie is often related to the consequence of discovery, or to the seriousness of deception. Western culture has this thing called a 'white lie', white implying good or at least forgiveable, whereby we evade guilt on the grounds that the lie is for the best. Our body language rarely gives us away if our mind has let us off the 'guilt' hook. As adults we may even employ the childish pseudo-

Top left: Although her open palms suggest that she is truthful her awkward body posture and strained expression imply an inner tension which may be caused by dishonesty.

Top right: Some people close their eyes as they lie in order to avoid the listener seeing deception in their 'windows to the soul'. A lopsided smile often gives away insincerity as well.

Bottom left: Her relaxed stance, natural, balanced smile and open body posture all suggest that she is telling him the truth.

Bottom right: In adults, touching the mouth can indicate anxiety, particularly in relation to recent or imminent speech.

magical trick of crossing our fingers as we tell a lie, hiding them behind our backs as we do so in order to avoid detection.

Here are the body language facts about lying to help you interpret your intuitive reactions to the photographs on the previous page, which were probably all quite easy to assess. However, it is important to remember that none of the following non-verbal signals are in themselves actual proof of deception. All of them can be caused by other psychological states or physical pressures, but they do tend to be associated with deception and if two or more of them occur simultaneously you should take it into consideration that a person may be lying to you.

Assuming that people are scared as they lie (which is a big assumption), their automatic nervous system will cause them to sweat more, particularly in the palms, which may become itchy. Breathing becomes uneven, throat and lips become dry, and swallowing may increase in frequency. The frightened liar generally talks less, speaking more slowly than usual, choosing words with care yet making more speech errors such as slips of the tongue, malapropisms, etc. There might be blushing, twiddling of pens or other objects, doodling, and an avoidance of physical contact as if in anticipation that the person being lied to might be able to feel the dishonesty emanating from the liar's body.

The inner conflict that takes place when we lie prompts a series of subtle but perceivable twitches, micro gestures, and facial movements that flash across the face in under a second. We notice these gestures, though we are often not consciously aware that we have done so. People who are lying often exhibit minute nervous ticks in the muscles of their mouths, usually only on one side, and in their cheeks or eyelids. They may

Below: 'There's lipstick on your collar!' An assumption of guilt may be as much an indication of a troubled relationship or a jealous nature as it is a reasonable response to apparently incriminating evidence of infidelity. Many people experience feelings of guilt when faced with hostile accusations, even if they are in reality quite innocent. Guilt-fed anxiety may in turn lead to non-verbal signals that are usually associated with dishonesty. However, in this case the man looks truly shocked at his girlfriend's discovery.

Right: His intense eye contact and hurt look at being accused suggest that he is telling the truth; they also signal a possible counter-attack. Would his body language make you believe him?

lying with the automatic mouth clamp, but the action is slowed. This slowing allows our brain to interrupt the natural process, overriding it by diverting our hands to a site nearby – most often the edge of the mouth, the nose (especially the underside), the cheek or the chin. This delay may range from a couple of seconds to as much as a minute. People sometimes wipe the mouth with a downward open palm gesture, as if to clean away guilt induced by their conscience.

Is honesty therefore always a better option? Well, yes, in that you will probably be caught out by the person you are lying to anyway – although they may choose not to let on or even to acknowledge this insight to themselves – but on the other hand maybe no, as the social conventions of politeness, flirtation and flattery sometimes oblige us to compliment or deceive in order to boost confidence or avoid obvious insult. If your date asks you if you like his suit you would do better to not tell him you think it stinks, especially if you know that he has gone to a lot of trouble to look nice for you. (However, if he asks you if he has bad breath you will be doing both of you a favour if you tell him the truth!)

If you do need to tell a lie, make it a convincing one: keep your hands animated and your body flexible, but not squirming or fidgety. Position both feet firmly on the ground and keep your voice as alive in expression as always. Otherwise you'll be giving yourself away, no matter how credible your words might be!

Finally, always bear in mind that the significance of eye contact differs from culture to culture. As you will see in the next chapter, you cannot assume that because someone is not looking you in the eye they are therefore withholding the whole truth or being downright dishonest.

also blink faster too, their eyebrows may twitch – again usually on one side – and their shoulders may move slightly.

Of course, a still photograph does not give the whole picture, as it is movement that betrays a lie. As we saw in Chapter 2, someone who is lying will often fidget, drum the fingertips, or entwine the fingers together. Toes will flex inside shoes, and the feet, especially if they are hidden from view, may tap agitatedly.

Most importantly, we almost always seem to revert to the childhood habit of taking our hands to our mouths as soon as a lie is spoken. The response is similar to that of a child revealing a big secret, realizing that he has blundered, then grasping at the invisible words as if they were still floating on the air, capable of being stuffed back into the offending orifice from which they have so recently sprung.

As we develop a more sophisticated control over the tell-tale body language that landed us in trouble when we were children we still respond to

THE EYES HAVE IT

As infants, we express many of our needs and desires exclusively through our eyes. This facility is something we never lose. The eye skills we learn at this early stage in our lives are critical in establishing and maintaining bonds with other people. Just think about these descriptive phrases: smouldering eyes; icy stare; looking daggers; if looks could kill; shifty eyes; deep eyes; the green-eyed monster; eyes of an angel;

piercing blue eyes; sheep's eyes; bedroom eyes; giving someone the evil eye or the glad eye. Think of certain film stars just by name and their eyes probably are the first thing you think of – for example, Omar Sharif, Peter O'Toole and Bette Davies.

The eyes are the most important tools in the successful use and understanding of sexual non-verbal communication. They are highly attuned ultra-sensitive sensory organs, shown by psychologists to be 18 times more sensitive than our ears, as measured by the relative size of the optic and cochlear nerves. They are vital both as receptors of non-verbal sexual signals, and as sensual communicators, capable of transmitting intimate covert and overt messages straight into the consciousness of other people. Note the following extracts:

The power of a glance has been so much abused in love stories that it has come to be disbelieved in. Few people dare now say that two beings have fallen in love because they have looked at each other. Yet it is in this way that love begins and in this way only. The rest is only the rest, and comes afterwards. Nothing is more real than these great shocks, which two souls give each other in exchanging this spark. **Victor Hugo, Les Miserables**

Above and right*: Our eyes give away our innermost secrets. They can communicate attraction and desire and even over distance we can sense when someone is watching us. But have you ever experienced love at first sight? Opinions differ as to the reliability and longevity of such instantaneous attraction, yet it is a phenomenon which seems to strike at the very heart of many and which is celebrated in folklore, mythology and love songs.*

Above: *Our eyes and the muscles surrounding them portray many expressions and moods. Look at the faces in the three photographs on this page and opposite, concentrating particularly on the eyes, and see what mood they evoke in you. What emotion do you feel each pair of eyes is portraying? The sad and soulful eyes in the picture above are characterized by the lowered upper lids, the lowered angle of the face, making the irises and pupils appear towards the top of the eye socket, the slightly creased forehead and slightly raised eyebrows.*

Right: *Feelings of both anger and disapproval are characterized by a piercing stare. As anger increases the eyebrows are drawn down like hoods over the eye sockets, the muscles below the eyes tighten and the eyes themselves appear to darken.*

Far right: *The message is clear: fearful and shocked eyes are instantly identifiable by the wide- eyed glare. A large proportion of the eyeball is revealed as the muscles surrounding the eyes are all pulled tight on the face. The eyebrows lift up and the lines on the face crease up in a reverse direction to that found in an expression of sadness.*

The eyes do not lie. They are, some say, the windows to the soul. The more you point others to your eyes, or allow other people access to the secrets they contain, the more truthful you are being, the more confident you feel and appear, and the more encouragement you give others to access your inner thoughts, feelings and desires.

HOW WELL DO YOU KNOW YOUR OWN EYES?

Take 10 minutes to examine your eyes carefully. Find a mirror (preferably one that magnifies the image), make yourself comfortable and position a bright lamp to one side of you so that your eyes are fully illuminated. The light will cause your pupils to contract. Have a close look at their colours – you may be surprised by the extensive but minute variety of colour speckles across the surface. Drink in all the tiny details, and imprint the image on your mind. Then close your eyes, turn off the light and wait for 30 seconds. In the darkness your pupils will dilate. Then open your eyes and watch carefully when you turn on the light again. How fast they change!

Try making different expressions with just your eyes. If you like, use a piece of cloth or card to conceal all of your face below the line of your eyes. Try anger, rage, sadness, joy, surprise, pleasure, shock, cunning, blatant sexuality . . . have fun exploring the power of your eyes.

Test yourself out on these three photographs. What do they say to you? Compare your intuitive responses with the points that are made in the accompanying captions.

Now study other people's eyes in real-life situations. Sit in your local bar for a while and observe what people do with their eyes. See how young couples in love spend minutes on end gazing deeply into each other's eyes. Watch how people flirt, 'making eyes' at each other, see how someone waiting for a date glances nervously at his or her watch. Notice whose eyes are scanning the room

and whose eyes seem about to pop out of their sockets in eager anticipation every time the bar door swings open. See how eyes flick down in disappointment, their owner's hopes dashed, when it is a stranger rather than the longed-for person who enters the room.

Let's examine some of the psychological secrets that researchers have discovered about the eyes. Look at the two photographs on the following pages and see which face you find most attractive. Michael Argylle, one of the world experts in this field, has shown that the larger our pupil size the more interested we are in what we are looking at, and that this is also a direct indicator of sexual interest and arousal. His research confirms experiments by Hess in the early 1970s which showed that men found photographs of women more attractive when the pupils were dilated. Likewise, women experience the same reaction.

Thus one of the completely uncontrollable sexual signals we all display is the dilation of our pupils. Italian women in the 18th century would place tiny drops of belladonna (an extract from the deadly nightshade plant) into their eyes to artificially dilate their pupils and increase their sex appeal. While this technique may be a little impractical in the late 20th century, all is not lost. The inventor of the wonderful electric light dimmer switch has much to be thanked for. Setting a romantic mood by turning down the lights partly achieves its success through the resultant pupil dilation which makes us appear simultaneously attractive and more turned-on. It has exactly the same effect on our companion. This is why candle-lit dinners are synonymous with romance – candle light is not only flattering to skin colour and texture, it encourages and shows off our pupil dilation to best effect.

Here's another secret: there is some evidence to suggest that under certain circumstances our emotional state may be influenced by our bodily state. For example, on finding your hands suddenly very clammy, you might subconsciously ask yourself, 'Are my hands sweating because I'm nervous, or am I nervous because my hands are sweating?' If the latter is true – and it makes sense – your brain looks for rational attribution of meaning to any physical response. Thus, given that your pupils will dilate in low light, your brain may rationalize this (subconsciously, of course) along the following lines: 'Aha! I notice my eyes are dilated. I'm having a nice time . . . I'm really quite interested in this person chatting to me . . . in fact I'm quite attracted to him/her.'

for the colour of their pupils and the shape of their eye surrounds. In Western culture almond-shaped eyes are particularly prized.

Especially in a babyish face, large eyes are the single best predictor of initial attraction between people of the opposite sex. This is why one of the central skills of eye flirting is to know how to make the eyes slightly larger without staring.

Left and right: Allow your eyes to dart backwards and forwards between these two photographs of a young woman. At first glance they may seem identical, but whether you are male or female you will almost certainly find one of the two images much more attractive than the other. Take note of which of the two sets of eyes you are more drawn to gaze upon. In fact the images are exactly the same except that the pupils in the right-hand picture have been enlarged. In a real-life setting this dilation of the pupils, which is beyond our control, occurs when we are attracted towards someone. Of course, bright light does cause the pupils to contract and therefore reduces the effect so if you are planning a romantic date a candlelit dinner is a good option.

MAKING THE MOST OF THE EYES

Ever since the time of the ancient Greeks and Egyptians cosmetics have been used, particularly by women, to enhance the size, shape and colour of the eyes. Make-up is used in modern and primitive cultures all over the world to make the skin appear more youthful and the eyes more beautiful. Many legendary film stars have been celebrated

Researchers allege that wearing glasses makes people less attractive, but this need not necessarily be the case. Glasses suit some people very well, in which case they can be used as a beauty prop rather than a screen to hide behind. However, do not wear dark glasses (especially the mirrored type) if you want to communicate non-verbally with any success. Hiding your eyes robs other people of the principal factors by which they judge whether they like you or not.

THE EYES HAVE IT

Some lenses magnify the eyes. Other people prefer the benefits of contact lenses, and even resort to the vanity of coloured lenses. These can have a startling effect, especially when used to enhance an existing colour in the blue/green spectrum. Other people are lucky enough to possess eyes of an unusual colour. Bright green eyes are especially rare and subsequently mesmerizing, as are eyes

whose irises include patches of a different colour contrasting with the main iris colour.

You will have noticed just how important the eyes are in non-verbal communication if you have ever conversed with someone who has two different-coloured eyes or a wandering eye. Confusion immediately sets in, as the normal unspoken conventions are broken and the brain has to struggle to understand the ambiguous eye signals that it is receiving.

SMILING EYES

As we shall see later, smiling is a key skill in successful seduction. It is possible to smile with just your eyes, in the same way that it is possible for us to hear when a person is smiling while speaking to us on the telephone. When speaking face to face we can also detect tiny changes in the many muscles around the eyes when a person smiles 'inside' his or her head. Our eyes seem to become brighter when we smile; they seem to sparkle. The facial changes may be very slight but we can detect the subtlest movement, and we respond subconsciously by feeling more attracted to that person.

The fact is that people will be more attracted to you the more you use your eyes to send out and react to unspoken messages. You will be perceived as being a more sympathetic, more expressive and more interesting person.

CUPID'S ARROWS

The eyes can be used to project clear messages, and the force of your personality too, over considerable distances and in very short spaces of time. Eyes can meet briefly across a railway station or even at red traffic lights. Until recently, the theatre was a classic venue for flirting from box to box or box to stalls, and included the use of binoculars and fans to send a great many sexual signals in a sort of subtle semaphore. These days, it is easy to glance in your driving mirror and meet the reflected eyes of the driver behind. Such a tiny exchange can make the heart beat faster and, at its most extreme, can cause the iciest-hearted to feel as if they have just been kicked in the chest by a mule. Just a few seconds later we go our different ways for ever: this is what psychologist Andrew Evans refers to as 'the myriad love affairs that never happen'.

Poets and novelists have for centuries described coming under the spell of someone's looks, being bewitched and mesmerized by a single glance. We really do seem capable of catching a potential lover with just our eyes. It can happen in the most unexpected places: in church; passing each other on a moving escalator; across a crowded bar; in the supermarket check-out queue . . .

So many people have regrets of missed opportunities. They fail to follow up the exchange of the initial spark, they often glance away without even returning an eyebrow flash, and then the moment has passed. If someone starts an eye conversation with you and you like their look, then answer back. You have a lot to gain and little to lose.

WHAT NEXT?

After the first burst of eye contact both parties naturally avert their gaze quite swiftly – this is part of the peek-a-boo phenomenon that is described in Chapter 6. What is important is that when you break the initial contact you do so by looking down. Glancing away in any other direction is less friendly, less inviting, less sexy. If you don't look away at all you can place a considerable amount of pressure upon the other person. A look that is too intense may be misconstrued as hostile.

If you have proceeded according to custom you may now go on to meet eyes again, scanning your target lover's eyes a couple of times and then scanning their face. They will probably scan your face similarly. Competently and sensitively done, this mutual scanning can be very pleasing, but it is easy to over-scan and to stare, which is very unpleasant, especially for women.

A clear scanning image pattern is shown by the experimental tracing of eye movements. Imagine that your eyes project two red laser-beams focused to a single point, a red dot, then imagine that wherever that dot moves, a tracer line is left. If scanning a face in a typical social setting left a visible trace, the pattern would be as is shown in the illustration on this page.

Our eyes dance backwards and forwards between the eyes and then include the mouth in a sweeping triangle movement with less frequent and wider sweeps to the extremities of the face and hair, building up a complete frame of reference that is centred on the eyes and mouth. Seventy-five per cent of the scan, or even more, is devoted to exploring the eyes and mouth. A normal face scan lasts about three seconds but, as with so many of the eye's sexual signals, a slight extension in duration to about four and a half seconds intensifies the emotional arousal of both parties. In the absence of any other visual cues, prolonged eye-to-eye contact is aggressive and will put the other

Right: Spend three minutes looking at this man's face. Your eyes do not stay fixed in one place but rather scan the whole face. See if you notice that your eyes keep returning to his eyes and mouth.

Left: The lines on the photograph show how a face might be scanned.

person on their guard even if they do not know why. Therefore, if you are going to extend eye contact, remember to smile a gentle, sincere smile (see Chapter 7) and accompany this with open, non-threatening hand and body signals (see Chapters 9 and 10).

A variety of cultural differences exist in all areas of non-verbal communication including eye-talk and should be taken into consideration, particularly if you live and socialize in a cosmopolitan setting. North American, British, and most European and Jewish cultures approve of direct eye-to-eye contact and actively encourage it as a sign of confidence and strength, whereas in Oriental and West Indian cultures eye-to-eye contact tends to be avoided. In a few countries (Korea, for example), any eye contact between a man and a woman is seen as potentially sexual and is therefore politely avoided, if at all possible. Other research has shown that Hispanic women tend to hold the eye-to-eye gaze of men for three seconds longer than other European women do – which can subsequently leave men feeling heartily rebuffed after they have believed that they were being 'given the eye'.

shoes, as well as details like wedding rings and other jewellery or watches. If they want to be more overtly sexual they spend more time eyeing a man's crotch. Often a man's behind is of particular importance as a turn-on, but many men's trousers hide their buttock muscles so the woman is left to use her imagination, basing her speculation on

FULL BODY SCANS

Women and men tend to scan each other's bodies differently. Women who are flirting are far more subtle in the way they scan a man's full image. They spend much more time on his face (especially the mouth and eyes), his hair and his overall size and build. They also scan his clothes, particularly

what is visible. For some women the length of a man's legs is also important, but this is not nearly as much of a visual turn-on as the length of a woman's legs is for men.

Women are all too often confronted with gawking men who virtually commit eyeball assault. It is humiliating, derogatory and unsexy for a woman to be 'undressed' by a stranger's eyes. Men seem to be instinctively over-assertive and often offensive with their eyes. It is far more flattering and pleasing for a woman to be admired in the manner she would adopt when admiring a man.

Women often feel that men simply have conversations with their chests, from the way men's eyes signal intent. The breasts exert a powerful draw. So do long legs, which send out a strong non-verbal sexual signal for men. The reason seems to be that as teenage girls mature towards full sexual potential they undergo a disproportionate spurt of growth in their legs. Hence the pressure on women

to increase their leg length artificially with high heels, and the fashions for shorter skirts which reveal greater leg length to give the impression of budding sexuality. With the advent of tight leggings and trousers it is even harder for men to resist ogling the sexual gender signals displayed by such clothing, but they should try to at all costs.

Once committed to a sexual relationship with a man a woman may enjoy turning him on and seeing his eyes drink in her sexuality, but not until a clear sexual bond has been formed should such overt 'red-dotting' be undertaken, and then only with the woman's clear consent The tendency of a man when meeting a woman is to scan her from the ground up, feet first and then legs, followed by crotch, torso, breasts, shoulders and face. The

whole scan takes a second or less but is very off-putting and unpleasant for the woman concerned. If practised in the workplace, it may even play a part in litigation over sexual harassment.

In fact the human eye is so keenly attuned that if someone begins to take a visual interest in us, say from across the room at a party, we will immediately take detailed mental notes not only of how their eyes connect and disconnect with ours, but also how their eyes are behaving the rest of the time. Many men blow their chances of

Left: We have the ability to detect even the briefest glance from someone sizing us up. One of the biggest causes of unease in women is when someone's gaze falls onto their breasts. In response a woman will often automatically adjust her clothing slightly to cover herself up. Men are particularly careless in the way they allow their eyes to wander in an obvious way. Not only is it unpleasant for the woman being 'eyeballed', it also makes the perpetrator look very unattractive to an onlooker and is unlikely to achieve positive results.

connecting with a potential partner because after the initial eye-to-eye contact has been made they get a severe case of 'wandering eye', where they scan every other female in the room with the same searing red dot that the first woman might have thought was exclusively for her. 'And I thought he only had eyes for me,' she might mutter to herself before adding one more to the junk pile of male rejects. Once in a relationship, both men and women (but women especially) seem to develop an uncanny sense which enables them to detect even the merest sideways glance at another attractive member of the opposite sex. The fact that this causes such distress to their partner is further evidence of the powerful sexual communication potential of our eyes.

THE EYES HAVE IT

THE EYEBROW FLASH

Our eyebrows help to frame the eyes and give sharp definition to signals we send with our eyes by accentuating any movement of the surrounding muscles. When we first see somebody across a room to whom we are attracted, we respond automatically with an eyebrow flash when that person looks our way. The whole event normally lasts about a fifth of a second during which our eyebrows will rise and fall, followed instantly by a

Right: The eyebrow flash is an instantly recognized non-verbal signal of friendly greeting practised in every corner of the globe. Because it is so universal, researchers claim that this gesture is an inborn response. As the eyebrows rise to their peak the eyeballs are exposed because the eyelids lift and the muscles around the eyes stretch, allowing more light onto the surface of the eyes. This makes them appear large and bright and is very attractive. The eyebrows are full of expression and essential for communicating a change of mood. Actors, clowns and mime artists alike spend hours practising specific movements of the eyebrows.

return eyebrow flash from the other person. This unifyingly human event is duplicated in every culture on earth. Its duration may be extended up to a second for deliberate effect.

An eyebrow flash is only employed when we wish to acknowledge another's presence, as it is a precursor to an exchange. An unwelcome eyebrow flash is easily ignored or even contradicted by pulling the eyebrows into a disapproving frown. Eyebrow flashes are also used in conjunction with a roll of the eyes to indicate exasperation, but the duration of the flash is usually longer than the warm 'greeting' flash.

In any potentially friendly exchange or meeting you should learn to initiate an eyebrow flash and be aware that returning an eyebrow flash across a

room will send a clear message of good intent. Unfortunately, some spectacle frames hide the eyebrows and some fair-haired individuals have near-invisible eyebrows which makes spotting the flash difficult. Range is important, too. At a distance of less than five feet the flash takes on a less agreeable feel. At 14 feet the other person may not see your flash, and under certain lighting conditions, particularly at a night-club or disco, you may fail to catch the eyebrow flash even when you are at the optimum distance.

TO STARE OR TO GAZE

Staring and gazing are not at all the same thing: one is attacking and the other inviting. A stare is like shooting invisible arrows from your eyes and into the eyes of the person on the receiving end, leaving them cold and defensive or feeling invaded. A gaze, however, welcomes a person into our line of sight, and into our eyes. The person upon whom we gaze feels great warmth. Women generally gaze more than men. This may be because they are often more attentive listeners, too, and the two often go together. Women will find the eyes of a man who gazes well very attractive, the more so because many men are unskilled at this.

GAZING FOR BEST EFFECTS

When you meet someone in whom you are interested, look them in the eye as they begin to speak. When they want you to speak they will probably pause for a moment. The expression around the eyes will change too. Don't ignore the pause signal – it is a cue for you to pick up the conversation. Intimacy develops with a deft response. The most

Above: The contrast between staring and gazing is dramatic. When we fix our eyes upon someone else our stare is characterized by an intensity and coldness that often indicates negative emotions or great fear. When we gaze our whole face is softer. The eyes appear gentle, inviting and welcoming of a friendly response.

'mutual lovers gaze' with someone who is a relative stranger if you can successfully draw another's look into the centre of your own eyes.

Women generally find doing this much simpler, as men are easy prey to a deep, hypnotic gaze. Give any man a dreamy, five-second burst of gazing and his toes will curl, his heart will flush, and he will become putty in a woman's hands.

When men try the same thing they usually blow it, because they stare. They come on with a visual onslaught far too strong. If a woman is shy or wary of intimate eye contact, the last thing she needs is for a man to look at her even more; it will frighten her. A man in this case should back off instead, turn the eye-heat right down, copy the woman's more furtive eye glances, enjoy the hide-and-seek game of sneaked looks and flashing glances, and build up slowly to the long gaze.

We make ourselves even more inviting by using the hands as pointers to draw the gaze of another person into our own gaze path. The pointer can be floating in mid-air, or actually touching our face, and doesn't have to be our fingers or hands – we can also point with pens and cigarettes, with pipes or glasses. Eyes automatically follow a moving hand, locking onto the powerful 'magnet' signal being beamed out from the centre of our eyes.

Much of human motivation is based on reward and fulfilment. Classical models of reinforcement show that it is possible to highlight another person's impression of us as attractive and sexy by reinforcing eye contact with something else pleasurable. So, for example, as we point to our eyes we should also smile, and if circumstances allow for it, say something flattering about the person upon whom we have fixed our eyes. If you are blessed with the ability to make others laugh, then do so as you point to your eyes for maximum reinforcement. The person upon whom your attention is fixed will experience a warm feeling inside and associate that feeling with a direct and intimate connection with you.

No matter what your expression may be, your eyes possess great power and influence. When you have finished reading this chapter, your increased awareness of your eyes will have increased their

effective gaze pattern is to do regular furtive glances with intervals of about three to five seconds between, increasing to every two to three seconds as interest develops.

We know that two people in love spend ages gazing into each other's eyes. They are unconsciously reading each other's pupil dilations and reaching for the deeper, perhaps intuitive secrets contained in such a personal exchange. You can take steps to bring about this highly desirable power. As soon as you can, get out onto the university of the street and you will see for yourself the immense sexual allure of the eyes.

BLINKS AND WINKS

Every time we blink we remoisturize the surface of our eyes. The rate at which we blink has a profound unconscious effect on anyone looking at or into our eyes. Just think for a minute of the excitement and tension (and often arousal) that takes place in you when you play the 'staring game'. Especially popular with children, this is a simple contest in which the first person to blink or avert their eyes is the loser. If you have not played the game for years, do so at the earliest opportunity and take note of how you feel the longer you hold out without blinking.

As small babies, it appears we need to blink less. As adults we blink once every two to three seconds, on average. If we don't think consciously about it our lids move at a very fast rate. Normally we don't notice our own or other people's blink rates. If the norm is diverted from, however, our supersense detects it immediately. For example, when the actor Robert Powell played Jesus Christ in Franco Zeffirelli's film *Jesus of Nazareth* he trained himself not to blink at all when his eyes were in shot. The effect was amazing – his eyes seemed to have beams of light blazing from them.

In marked contrast, some people close their eyes for extended periods of time during conversation. Desmond Morris labelled this phenomenon as 'cutoff' behaviour. Someone doing this excludes all visual stimulation, and in so doing excludes anyone who might wish to communicate with them, which can be insulting and unattractive.

To induce a romantic feel, however, by all means blink. If someone looks at us eye-to-eye and is very attracted to us, not only will that person's pupil size increase, so will their blink rate. You can increase the blink rate of the person to whom you are talking by blinking more yourself; if the person likes you he or she will unconsciously try to match your blink rate to keep in synchrony

with you. This will in turn make you both feel attracted to each other. Eyelashes focus the gaze upon the eyes, which is why the fluttering eyelash is considered so flirtatious and why men with very long or very dark eyelashes are often considered very attractive by women.

When a blink mimics a wink it becomes very sexual without being corny or ogling. It's what I call the two-eyed wink. This is done by blinking in slow motion, consciously slowing down the rate of your blink to a half or a third of the natural speed. Both men and women seem to find the effect very attractive. It is especially potent if done as follows. Let us imagine the protagonist is male. He starts by looking away from the female he wishes to flirt with. When he senses she is looking at him, he casts his eyes towards hers, slowly meeting her gaze. He holds still for about three seconds, then blinks very slowly and then smiles as he reopens his eyes. He waits for her to smile in response and then looks away again. The whole sequence has lasted about seven seconds.

A woman tends to look in a man's direction, or directly into his eyes, in short, furtive glances. Her eyelashes can be used to dramatic effect, as they enhance the apparent size of the eye and exaggerate the provocative fluttering of the eyelids. Men normally gaze for longer periods of time. However, they would do well to learn to mimic the more feminine visual approach.

The wink proper is a fantastically powerful sexual signal when it is employed by women, but is often something of a turn-off when used by men. The 'nudge, nudge, wink, wink' overtones of men sharing a lurid joke is a sad perversion of the original meaning we learn in childhood when a knowing wink signifies a shared secret, something special and thrilling because of its covert quality. Men can use winks to send a clear message of sexual intent towards a woman, but they are best delivered with subtlety. The 'quieter' the wink, the more pleasing it is to receive. Delivered in conjunction with a gentle smile it can be devastating.

As with most non-verbal sexual signals, women are more skilled at delivering such messages. A wink from a woman can have a dramatic effect

THE EYES HAVE IT

Below: *The fantastic sexual appeal of long eyelashes is shown dramatically here by artificial lashes. Allow your eyes to glance backwards and forwards between the twins' eyes and see how you are continually more attracted to the face of the one on the left. Long eyelashes act like a pair of wide-open arms irresistibly inviting your gaze into the very centre of the welcoming pupils.*

upon a man. He will usually interpret the signal as an overt invitation, so it should be used with care.

One of the most erotic ways to touch someone early in an intimate encounter is to give them 'butterfly kisses'. This is when you gently caress the cheek and maybe the nose of the other person with the tips of the eyelashes of one eye. Try it now on the palm of your hand if you've never tried it before. It's a lovely, soft, tickling feeling.

Your eyes are your most precious assets in the armoury of signals available to you when applying the secrets of attraction, so use them wisely!

CHAPTER SIX

PEEK-A-BOO

Peek-a-boo is one of our first and favourite games in life and it is reflected in many adult non-verbal sexual signals. As babies we experience a disproportionate degree of pleasure when adults tease us by alternately hiding and revealing their eyes. Infants rarely tire of the game, squealing and giggling with delight every time the eyes reappear as if by magic. Peek-a-boo is also one of the first games we learn as

infants which teaches us the excitement of anticipation. The longer the eyes are concealed the greater the tension and the more pleasurable the relief when concealment is removed to reveal smiling eyes. The effect is similar to the interruption of the sun's warm rays by a passing cloud. The renewed pleasure of the sunlight is somehow increased by it having been temporarily denied us.

The 'now-you-see-me-now-you-don't' pleasure principle is one that continues throughout childhood, both with direct games of peek-a-boo and with hybrid versions, such as promising not to look and then peeking through slightly parted fingers, snapping them shut if it seems that we are about to be found out.

Understanding and applying the psychological effect of peek-a-boo in all areas of sexual communication is paramount to success in the secret world of non-verbal seduction. The two-eyed wink described in the previous chapter is so effective because it is a miniature peek-a-boo event. In adulthood peek-a-boo is seldom actually played with the hands, although a pleasurable derivative of it is to run up behind someone you know, put your hands over his or her eyes and spin him or her around after a quick 'guess who?' or 'surprise!'. Instead, we use other objects to deliberately interrupt our eye-line. In many romantic historical films actresses use their fans to dramatic sensual effect by hiding their eyes behind eyelash-like fluttering feathered fans, raising and lowering them provocative-

Above and right: We play peek-a-boo with potential suitors using myriad subtle gestures and movements in which other people or objects are manipulated to enable us to momentarily engage and disengage eye contact. Splits in clothes also allow the wearer to tease admirers by playing peek-a-boo where skin is substituted for eyes. The now-you-see-me-now-you-don't glimpses of flesh are a potent arouser.

74

ly. This movement, combined with the eyebrow flash and then the lowering of the eyes, can be breathtaking. The tension-relief effect is perhaps the principal agent of pleasure in seeing a bride lift her veil to reveal her face and eyes and there is a celebration of it at any masked ball, especially when hand-held masks are raised and lowered in a teasing cat-and-mouse manner.

But how do we play sexual peek-a-boo without fancy props and costumes? Imagine a contemporary setting. Mark and Anna sit at separate tables in the café of an art museum. She is studiously reading the show catalogue. He is reading the café menu. Their supersense radar will have already alerted each of them that there is a member of the opposite sex facing them, even though the distance between them is substantial and both have dining tables fortifying their positions.

Mark notices that Anna is very attractive and lowers his menu briefly to admire her with a face and body scan. She becomes aware of his eyes on her and glances over the top of her catalogue. Mark flicks his eyes back towards the lowered menu. This happens twice more in quick succession. The dance has begun. He lifts his menu and rests his elbows on the table so his eyes are in line with Anna's face, but blocked by the menu. He waits a good 10 seconds then tips the top edge of the menu towards her so as to reveal his eyes. Anna holds Mark's gaze for two seconds then pretends not to have noticed and returns with more vigour to reading her catalogue, quite unconvincingly. By now she has decided that she is quite attracted to this stranger and so goes out of her way to feign indifference. At that moment the waitress come to take Mark's order. He flashes a quick glance in Anna's direction to check if she is looking at him talking to the waitress. She is! He is pleased and she is mildly embarrassed to have been caught taking an interest.

Anna decides to turn up the heat in the game. She looks at Mark's face as she reaches for her coffee. She keeps her eyes on him as she lifts the coffee to her lips. He looks back and their gaze meets for a couple of seconds. Anna then deliberately tilts her cup to obscure Mark's eye-line. He

Above: *Catching someone's eye using an adult version of peek-a-boo is a delightful pastime. This man is sitting in an outside restaurant and is using his menu to play peek-a-boo with a woman at a nearby table. He could just as easily use a cup or glass or people who interrupt their line of vision to play his game. Peering around a menu in this way, establishing eye contact and then disappearing again can induce a feeling of merriment in both participants that is disproportionate to the actual event. Once eye contact has been made and smiles exchanged the non-verbal communication may proceed to conversation.*

PEEK-A-BOO

leans slightly forward and up to try to maintain contact. She knows she has got him if she wants and lowers her cup. Mark realizes he has been caught and smiles in recognition of Anna's skills. She smiles mildly back. He tilts his head slightly to one side and raises his eyebrows as if to ask a question. Anna smiles again and meets Mark's gaze directly, then she tilts her head slightly to echo his stance. Our players are both doing brilliantly. Not a word has yet been spoken but the two have participated in a delicious flirtation without obligation which will allow either of them to leave it at that without penalty. We need watch them no further.

Peek-a-boo can be played in any number of differing situations; on the train, peeking over a newspaper; in the library, over a book; in an art gallery, peering around the sides of a large piece of sculpture; in a disco or a bar, peeking around a pillar; even in a crowd, using other people to obscure the line of vision.

We can play peek-a-boo on the move too. As you walk down a street you can flash your eyes at someone, glance away and look back again. Sometimes the person will look back over his or her shoulder after passing by, doing a double-take.

Done well, peek-a-boo is harmless, sensuous, and can be downright sexy. Long hair is wonderful for masking an eye; it is then possible – and very alluring – to play peek-a-boo by covering and uncovering just one eye.

As you will see later, we can also use other parts of the body and even our clothes to play this game. This is why torn jeans can be sexy. Even across the knee, a tear in the material enables us to flash a tantalizing small surface area of flesh and then hide it again by shifting position in order to close the gap in the material. Tears in the seat of jeans are almost irresistible, the non-verbal message sent is so arousing.

So peek-a-boo can be exciting, arousing, entertaining, laugh-inducing, flirtatious and even highly erotic. You've probably been playing your own version of it for years and just never realized it. If you haven't, it is never too late to start!

Below: A momentary glance can be nearly as electrifying for the recipient as if he or she had been struck by two bolts of lightning! This woman is standing in a row of people at a bar. Everyone else is facing forward trying to attract the barman's attention but she turns her head and leans forward to glance along the bar to catch the eye of a man she would like to attract. She can easily disappear again by moving back so that the people who separate them will obscure her. Peeking around other people at someone you want to attract can be explosively provocative, for the desire to re-establish eye contact is well-nigh irresistible.

CHAPTER SEVEN

KISS AND TELL

Mouths are almost as complex as eyes. A disproportionately large percentage of our brain is allocated to interpreting signals from, and directing the behaviour of, our lips and tongue. We often define people's characters according to their mouths, describing them with expressions such as tight-lipped or mealy-mouthed, or as having a stiff upper lip, a false smile, a Bardot pout, a Cheshire cat grin, a sensuous mouth, hot lips and so on.

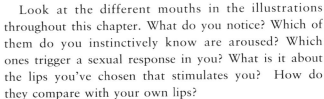

Look at the different mouths in the illustrations throughout this chapter. What do you notice? Which of them do you instinctively know are aroused? Which ones trigger a sexual response in you? What is it about the lips you've chosen that stimulates you? How do they compare with your own lips?

Examine your lips in a mirror. Are they narrow and colourless, fleshy and soft, firm and dark, or cracked and chapped? Are your lips quite evenly shaped or very asymmetrical? Do you bite them a lot, and if you do, does it look attractive when you do it? Are you a very mouth-oriented person? Do you touch your lips a lot with your fingers, or other objects like pens or cigarettes (the latter are often a turn-off when it comes to mouth sensuality). Do you love playing with chewing gum in your mouth? Do you get a lot of comfort from your mouth by biting your nails, sucking your thumb or gnawing a knuckle? Are you very sensuous when it comes to tasting your food and drink? Do you savour tastes in a sexual way? Have you learned to smell using your mouth and tongue as a powerful addition to your nose? These are all important questions designed to make you more aware of your own mouth and how important it is in receiving non-verbal sensuous and sexual signals and in sending them to other people.

Above and right: The mouth is central to sexual attraction and never more so than in the art of kissing. Everyone from Shakespeare and Byron to 20th-century lovesong lyricists has had something to say about kissing. Trading molten kisses is the first act of passion that delineates the boundary between non-sexual and sexual behaviour. People remember their first-ever romantic kiss, and the first time they kissed their present partner.

SMILES

It is often the mouth that gives away a person's real mood. A false smile is a dead give-away which is all too easily spotted. Smiles come in hundreds of forms and degrees of intensity, yet whether it is

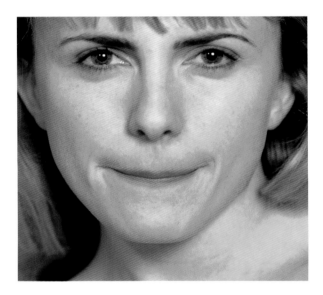

a big grin or a shy flicker of a smile we are somehow able to detect it when someone is not using the risorious muscle 12 – that is to say, when the feelings and thoughts in someone's head are not conducive to smiling. The insincere smile is given away most noticeably by asymmetry. The smile is one-sided, frequently looks exaggerated and is held in a fixed position for too long. The lower lip moves less than the upper, as if it had been frozen,

*At first glance these smiles may appear to be very similar, but look again more closely. Each conveys its own distinct message. See how the smile spreads across the face and eyes in some and not in others. **Above:** The closed-mouth smile, when natural, is used normally when we are smiling to ourselves. But here it is slightly lop-sided, which indicates insincerity.*

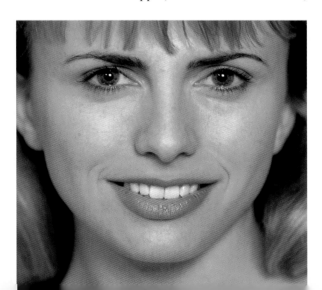

Above left: *The tight-lipped smile, also known as the miserable smile, often indicates suppressed anger or pain.* ***Above:*** *The full or broad smile is symmetrical. The laughter lines begin to appear on the face and around the eyes.* ***Left:*** *A false smile is indicated by the tight jaw and top lip, cold, slightly narrowed eyes and lack of laughter lines.*

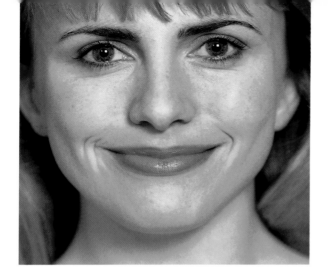

Above: During sexual arousal the lips swell and darken in colour. Coloured lipsticks simultaneously hide this natural change and mimic it; dark reds suggest a state of permanent arousal. *Right:* An exaggerated full-teeth smile can be hostile, especially when the teeth are clenched. Here the smile is also one-sided, like an insincere politician's smile.

Above: A genuine happy smile lights up the whole face. The eyes smile and sparkle, the cheekbones lift, the smile lines around the eyes and mouth are obvious and the jaw muscles are relaxed. Research shows that regular smiling can lift depression by releasing chemicals into the brain that change our mood. *Right:* The pouting smile is an overtly sexual invitation to a kiss.

and, most importantly, the eyes refuse to co-operate with the false actions of the lips.

A genuine smile activates not only the risorius muscle 12 but also the arbicularis oculi, the muscle that causes our cheeks to rise and draws in the skin around the eye-sockets, causing crinkling at

the outer corners of the eyes. The real smile is well-rounded, with happy lines extending out across the whole face, including the forehead, which becomes less creased, and the eyebrows, which flatten out or rise up.

Both men and women (but more so women) tend to bare their teeth as they become very aroused sexually. This expression of a primitive, aggressive, adrenalin-driven state of sexual arousal

links homo sapiens to the other primates. A tight-lipped or closed-mouth smile is less sensuous. A smirk or sly grin is an almost guaranteed turn-off, as is a very immobile smile.

To practise relaxing your face to make natural, symmetrical smiling easier, try scrunching up all your facial muscles as tight as you possibly can for five seconds and then relaxing them. Do this five times, then give yourself a face massage with the fingertips of each hand, using massage oil or face cream if you like. Take your time, covering the whole surface of your face with small circular motions. Concentrate especially on the forehead to get rid of worry wrinkles, on the temples to relieve pressure, and on the cheeks and muscles connected to your mouth.

Pleasurable thoughts tend to evoke smiles. You should never suppress a smile as it will be one of your most attractive assets, whatever your looks. We are automatically attracted to smiling faces and we smile back involuntarily in response to a smile greeting. You have the ability right now to make yourself more sexually attractive simply by choosing to smile more. The ability to make others smile and laugh is sexy. Part of our attraction motivation is naturally selfish; we like to imagine what the person we are eyeing up will bring us in terms of pleasure rewards. Smiling a lot scores very high on the unconscious pleasure-principle selection scoreboard.

Smiling has a dramatic effect on our feelings and our physiology. Just pulling our face muscles into a big smile makes us feel better. 'But won't that be a fake smile?' you might ask: the answer is yes and no! A fake smile held for long enough can actually make us feel more positive and think more optimistic and happy thoughts, which will in turn cause a real smile. The process can be thought-led too. By focusing your mind on a positive or funny smile-inducing thought to the exclusion of depressing thoughts you can bring a smile to your face.

Laughter is even more therapeutic and sexy than smiling. When you laugh you release a variety of natural drugs into the bloodstream that give pleasure and relaxation. The oft-reported case of the man who cured a terrible illness with laughing is worthy of retelling: Norman Cousins actually cured himself of the 'incurable' disease ankylosing spondylitis by watching hour upon hour of comedy films and having comic books read to him.

After a good laugh our bodies are in a state of arousal very similar to when we are sexually turned on: we breathe in and out very deeply and our blood circulation is heightened, causing the surface of the skin to blush. If you are going to take a first date to the cinema, choose a comedy – you will both come out looking flushed and turned on after a good laugh and will automatically feel more attracted to one another.

One of the principal reasons so many people fail in their attempts to use non-verbal communication to attract or impress members of the opposite sex is that, often without realizing it, they spend most of their time looking utterly miserable. Walk into any nightclub or disco and you will be greeted with endless stony faces. Anxious or miserable expressions are so unsexy. Men and women who take the whole business of attracting a mate very seriously have no fun at all and work themselves into such self-doubt that the vibrations they give off scream out the messages 'Back off', 'Keep clear', 'Don't bother, you'll have a miserable time with me', 'I hate myself.'

The man who bites his lower lip appears anxious. In contrast, a woman biting her lower lip can do so very alluringly. If she wants to go even further she can do so by slipping a finger into her mouth, approaching the obscene, but she does so at her peril as this is so provocative.

We are sometimes less skilled at smiling than we think, or are out of touch with the way our smile feels to us in contrast to the way it looks to others. If you watched video footage of yourself at a party taken by a hidden camera, you might be surprised to see that while you were feeling very content and thought you were smiling, your face appeared neutral or even downcast.

Stand in front of a mirror and do this small exercise. Close your eyes and smile. Imagine in your mind's eye how the smile will look, then open your eyes. Try this several times a day with different intensities of smiles, so as to become

Below: The smile as a warm greeting is as infectious as it is attractive. A glowing natural smile has a potent effect: it makes us feel better emotionally, more relaxed, more confident, more optimistic and hopeful. It makes the recipient or even passive witness of our smile feel good inside too. Combining a broad symmetrical smile with an open palm hand greeting sends a very warm non-threatening message. Adding open body language signals to this already winning combination makes us almost irresistibly attractive.

better acquainted with your own smile. You will get a better idea of the type of smile you may want to offer others.

Remember: if you smile at someone with your mouth and eyes, keep good eye contact for at least four seconds so that you really pack a punch.

LIP COLOUR

Pigments applied to the lips have been used to enhance feminine beauty for at least 5000 years. Men have also decorated their mouths over the millenia, but to nowhere near the extent that women have. As with the application of other cosmetics, colouring the lips sends a non-verbal signal of sexual arousal which evokes a particularly strong reaction in men. It is true that actual bodily

Above: Laughing is even more therapeutic than smiling. Research suggests that as little as one full minute of hearty laughter relaxes us for up to 45 subsequent minutes and many people who suffer from pain report relief after intense laughter. Anyone who has read the 'lonely hearts' ads in magazines will have noticed that most include the request that the potential respondent must have a good sense of humour. The ability to really laugh aloud and to make others laugh are both central ingredients of sexual attraction. The more you laugh the better you will feel and the more others will be attracted to you.

arousal in both men and women leads to more blood flowing to the lips, making them redder, yet in most cultures today it is only the women who wear lipstick, lending weight to the hypothesis that colouring the lips mimics the increased colouring that occurs in the female genitals when a woman is sexually aroused. The inner labia actually do become bright red just prior to orgasm.

WET LIPS

In the same way, wet lips seem to mimic the increased lubrication of the female genitals during sexual arousal. Thus many lipsticks are glossy to make the lips appear constantly wet, as if just licked. Licking the lips is at the extreme end of non-verbal sexual signalling with the mouth and tongue. When exaggerated or blatantly done, it looks lecherous and uninviting. Done subtly, it sends a clear unspoken message of attraction. The latter effect can be achieved by licking the lips while the other person is visually distracted or by employing one hand as a momentary shield to hide the lips for a moment as they are licked. A sensuous extension of this is to use a single finger like a lipstick applicator.

Alternatively, tasting food and drink provides the acceptable excuse for licking lips and gives ample opportunity for sending arousing signals to a potential paramour. Men have described being brought to a state of near orgasm simply by watching a woman eat certain foods suggestively, a fact well known to, and exploited unashamedly by, advertising agencies. The sensuality of many foods – particularly the texture and juiciness of certain fruits, for example – and the eating of food with the hands and the subsequent licking of the fingers allows for a full display of sexual confidence and competence. When we use our mouths like this we are virtually advertising our talents and hinting at what might be in store for a potential lover. There are many ways a woman can take food off her fingers, ranging from the highly erotic to the downright terrifying! Similarly, a man eating the meat off a chicken leg at a beach barbecue,

for example, can display a variety of signals, showing himself to be anything from a sensitive wet kisser and nibbler to a caveman-like chomper, showing promise of the possibilities ahead – or warning women off!

For demonstrating finesse, the most effective technique is the slight wetting of the lips using the darting tip of the tongue. For women who choose not to wear lipstick, and for men too, there are many products on the market that gloss the lips with moisture, including flavoured balms that anoint the lips with seductive aromas.

SWOLLEN LIPS

Whatever the shape of your lips, their volume increases when you become sexually aroused. Blood causes them to engorge, increasing their sensitivity dramatically as if preparing them for kissing, and again mimicking the genitals. A number of celebrated fashion models and actresses in the late 1980s had their lips injected with silicone in order to send a non-verbal signal of permanent sexual arousal. As with other artificial beauty-enhancing processes, this treatment has the detrimental effect of robbing women of choice. Remember, it is choice that gives us freedom and power and control over our sexual non-verbal communications. As discussed in Chapter 2, we are generally more skilled at controlling the muscles and signals of the face than those of the rest of the body, though control of the size of our lips is virtually impossible.

A KISS IS NEVER JUST A KISS

As we become attracted to someone our lips and mouth become increasingly sensitive to touch and other stimulation. Thus a man or woman standing at a bar eating a savoury snack will, without realizing it, take even bigger mouthfuls and chew faster as they become aroused. If they are smoking (which many people find a very unsexy habit), more drags will be taken on the cigarette. Next, people will actually touch their own mouths more, indicating that they may wish to speak to you and/or kiss you, as well as giving themselves pleasure by stimulating their ever-more sensitized and engorged lips.

A kiss is one of the most intimate and sensual non-verbal sexual signals that we have. The way we kiss someone the first time may have a direct effect on whether the relationship continues. Kisses are wonderful things when done well. They have substance (we blow them at people as if they could feel them land on their cheeks and lips), they have sound (we send kisses down telephone wires), they have incredible power.

Cultural differences certainly abound. Many Eastern European men still 'kiss' women's hands as a greeting, although they do not actually touch their lips on the back of the hand unless they intend to send an overt sexual signal. In the Middle East it is perfectly acceptable for men to kiss other men, and across Europe the number of times you 'kiss the air' each side of the face on exchanging greetings ranges from one to four.

What a difference it makes if you actually kiss someone's cheek when it is offered to you. Normally, if you are being introduced to someone at a social occasion you shake them by the hand, but on departing it is quite acceptable to kiss goodbye. Normally the kiss is to the air, but if it is to the cheek it is brief, about three-quarters of a second touching time. If you extend this touching time by just half a second to one and a quarter seconds the non-verbal message is clear: 'I fancy you and I want to kiss you lots more!'

It is important to proceed through the various developmental stages of kissing in order to feel not only turned on but at ease as intimacy develops. If you attempt to kiss someone full on the lips before he or she is ready, you may force him or her to retreat or turn awkwardly away, offering you a cheek at best. Alternatively, you may find yourself encountering a tightened jaw and tense lips.

Ideally, then, the progression starts out as follows: firstly kiss gently on the lips, mouth closed, then slowly let the kisses become firmer with the mouth still closed. Then part the lips slightly, as this allows you to smell each other's breath and taste each other's saliva, both of which carry a great deal of information, including secretions from the sebaceous glands which indicate the state of arousal. You can also feel the warmth of your co-kisser's breath. As the lips and tongue are very sensitive to temperature, warmth is a sure signal of sexual arousal. Cold skin and lips are an indication to slow down and back off.

The breath and saliva are important non-verbal messengers. Ideally you should offer the person you are going to kiss a biological message as unadulterated as possible. This is why smoking is so sexually unsavoury; it disguises the secrets of your desire. By the same token, this is why you should not use artificial breath fresheners, toothpaste or mouthwash just prior to kissing. All these disguise who you are sexually like a blanket dropped over your head. Also, many drinks (especially beers but some spirits too) serve only to throw the person we are kissing off the scent. The sebaceous glands located in the mouth and in the corners of the lips release semiochemicals which are highly sexually stimulating. The combination of this stimulation, which is very intoxicating and pleasurable, together with our own unique saliva 'fingerprint', is the most sensual way of exchanging personal credentials. We usually know if we are going to be suited to each other physically after the first full kiss.

What matters is that your teeth should be clean, and, especially, clear of rotting food (use dental floss). Your breath should be healthy and natural, which is usually the case if you are fit and healthy and haven't just feasted on garlic. (Chew fresh parsley to neutralize the effects of garlic.)

As passion increases we part our lips further, literally opening ourselves up to each other. Men tend to rush this stage in the kissing process, pushing their lips hard onto their partner's lips, sticking their tongue into her mouth, invading her body space. Male and female individual preferences vary greatly so you should not assume that someone likes to be kissed in the same way as you do. The strong, passionate kiss is a real turn-on for some people, but you should go gently and explore first

– your partner will show you by example how he or she likes being kissed if you allow the time for it. Tune your lips into your partner's and read what they are telling you. The messages can include: too fast; too strong; deeper; less pressure; more teeth; nibble my lower lip; suck my tongue; lick my teeth; play sword-fights with my tongue; make your tongue soft; make your tongue hard; show me how you will give me oral sex when we make love. All these different messages are possible and more.

If the eyes of a man or woman to whom you are attracted meet yours, his or her lips will automatically part for a moment if the attraction is mutual. This movement is often very subtle. At the extreme, someone who is very sexy can literally take your breath away!

Remember, don't hide your mouth, especially your smile. All too often we bring our hands up to cover our mouths, such as to stifle a laugh, and in doing so we hide one of our most precious assets. The eyes act as searchlights to pinpoint our gaze on others and as flares to attract attention. Once someone's eyes are upon you, direct their gaze into your eyes and towards your mouth and lips. All human beings scan faces in a triangular motion between the eyes and the lips, so do not interfere with this natural pattern. Use it to your advantage; do not hide your mouth, point at it instead.

It's easy to forget how important mouths are in sending non-verbal sexual signals as we are usually so preoccupied with the verbal messages we're using our mouths to communicate. But lips always speak louder than words!

CHAPTER EIGHT

HEADING FOR ROMANCE

Hold your head up and people look at you; slouch and they look away. The posture and orientation of the head and shoulders speaks volumes about your personality. The bearing of your upper body makes the difference between attraction and repulsion, either drawing people to you or pushing them away – something you may never have realized. Your head can shake, nod, circle, tilt, waver, bob or waggle.

With your shoulders and head you can weave and thrust, shudder or shiver. Your head can be stiff and awkward on your neck and shoulders, or appear free, relaxed and graceful.

The head serves as host to the eyes, ears, nose, mouth, and brain: that is, the complete control and sensory functions for the application of non-verbal sexual signalling. The face is the principal asset upon which we are judged by others as attractive or not, the principal stage upon which we act out our feelings and thoughts for others to see. The head is capable of numerous degrees of movement and angle, ranging from the tiniest, almost imperceptible nod to an exaggerated all-encompassing shake from side to side, so that our chin touches our shoulders.

If we are attracted towards someone we indicate this with our head. We turn our face towards them. We nod at them, and even if this is a very small movement it will be detected. It elicits a good response. If someone is talking to you, the more you respond to their speech with nods, the more they will be encouraged to continue talking, and the more they will enjoy being in your company. Many people find talking to strangers a strain; if someone experiences talking to you as easy or even pleasurable, they will be attracted towards you.

We point with our heads too, often in conjunction with numerous other face and hand gestures. We can indicate direction, or signal to someone that we are interested

Above and right: The upper back, shoulders, neck and head all play a part in attraction. Everything from the angle of the skull to the length, colour and texture of the hair affects perceived sexuality. Intimacy, trust and love are communicated by the neck snuggle of the couple above. The picture on the right shows that the neck, ears, face and scalp are very sensitive and can provide unexpected erogenous zones.

in further contact. Using head movements, we can determine whether the interest is mutual. The more relaxed and attractive the head movements, the more positive the answer will be. As we tend to store tension, anxiety and stress around the neck and shoulders, flexibility in these parts shows that a person is at ease. The person with a stiff posture is simply less sexy.

A head held in one fixed position is disconcerting. A chin stuck out or dropped low, a jaw too tightly clenched or grinding the teeth, a head tilted back too far will all suggest unattractive qualities and undesirability.

Early on in a verbal exchange people tend to over-nod to show their enthusiasm for another's company. Normally we nod in twos. If we nod three times in a row it sends the message that we want to say something back.

THE NECK

The neck is a more expressive part of our body than many of us realize. A stiff neck has a bad effect on our general sense of well-being, confidence and emotional arousal.

The neck is a vulnerable and sensitive area. The muscles surrounding the spinal cord need to be relaxed and correctly positioned for us to be most finely tuned to non-verbal communications. Fear is capable of making the hairs on the back of the neck literally stand on end. On the other hand, if we find someone very attractive our neck hairs will be soft and down-like, and we may experience a pleasurable tingling sensation too. Some women have an erogenous zone on their spine six vertebrae down from the skull. The author knows of one woman who would wear her pony tail at just the right length to be able to tickle her erogenous zone, and so quietly orgasm her way through the more tedious lectures at university. To invite someone to touch your neck shows trust and is very intimate. The neck is one part of us that we normally reserve for our lovers alone.

While we frequently lean forward towards someone we feel drawn to, another gesture of

sexual interest is to tilt the head back to reveal the neck and throat more openly. Both men and women do this, although men seem to respond more to the signal. The skin of the throat is often very soft and the rounded contours of the muscles mimic the more sexual areas of our bodies. Baring the throat may be the remnant of a primitive submissive gesture, seen in the behaviour of many animals, where the neck and belly are exposed in deference to a dominant member of the same species or a potential attacker. There is a possible link between this and the human male's sexual

Right: The neck display appears in many forms. Here a woman runs her fingers through her hair (a preening gesture) and tilts her head back to reveal the full extent of her neck from the tip of her chin to the line of the material of her dress. Meanwhile she is maintaining eye contact and smiling, all these signals indicating her attraction to the man. Her head is angled to one side, too, a flirtatious and often arousing position which also indicates that she is listening carefully to what he is saying.

appreciation of long necks. It is worth noting that many women's clothes are fashioned to highlight or enhance neck length.

THE EARS

This may sound ridiculously obvious, but before anything else make sure they are clean. Imagine that at a party you have been getting on really well with a person you fancy. You agree enthusiastically to the invitation to a slow dance. Everything is going well, then you happen to glance into your dance partner's ear to be greeted with a little nest of dirt. Would you still fancy him or her?

Apart from cleanliness, and a dab of moisturizing cream to the skin now and then if the outer parts are dry, you should not worry about the physical appearance of your ears. Everyone's ears are different and there are no fixed stereotypes for sexy ears. What does matter is how you use them.

The greatest simple communication skill is that of being a good listener. It is the non-verbal response to speech. It is a pity that men are apt to talk mainly about themselves when trying to make a good impression on women they find attractive. They also frequently talk at, rather than with, the woman and while they may ask questions they then demonstrate lack of interest in her views by ignoring the answers.

Your ears have a vital role to play in seduction, so use them as much as you can. They will bring you plenty of information about the person you are listening to, both in terms of verbal and non-verbal language. At least 30 per cent or more of our understanding of what people say depends on the sound of their voice, rather than on the words that are actually spoken. Paralinguistics is the study of the non-verbal aspects of speech, and research in this area shows that we make many assumptions about a person from the tone, speed, breathiness and musicality of the voice – including how sexy the person is. Our ears also bring us information on a partner's breathing rate, and from this we are able to synchronize with them better.

In order to indicate that you are listening closely to someone, it helps to tilt your head to one side. The more in tune we are with someone the more we copy their movements, including the angle of tilt of their head. A woman who is sexually attracted to a man will unconsciously tilt her head forwards and to the side. If this movement is combined with sideways eye glances, this sends a very strong sexual signal. A man taking the initiative can take up this head position so as to elicit a mirroring response from the woman, thus setting in motion the subconscious feelings of attraction.

The actual proximity of our heads also speaks volumes. As we grow more intimate with someone our desire to bring our faces closer together increases. The effect is two-fold: we exclude all other distraction from our field of vision and

unconsciously prepare for our first kiss, which is the opening of a major chapter in the sexual development of any relationship.

As our faces come into closer proximity the design of our eyes means that we will only be able to focus clearly on one part of the other person's face: the most intimate pre-kiss position possible is where our eyes are aligned with each other and are clearly in focus. It is probably for this reason that we often close our eyes when we actually kiss; the visual information has become redundant, and by closing our eyes we are better able to concentrate on the feel, smell and taste of the kiss.

HAIR

Facial hair appears in earnest during adolescence, with growth accelerated by male sex hormones. Most women have some limited facial hair; excess facial hair sends an ambiguous non-verbal sexual signal to men. Men's facial hair tends to be very

rough and can be painful for women when kissing. Individual preferences in the aesthetics of facial hair varies enormously. Some women love men with beards or moustaches; most seem to regard clean-shaven men as sexier, although designer stubble is regarded by others as rugged, masculine and, therefore, attractive.

Individual and cultural differences exist with regard to body hair too. Some cultures favour women who are almost hairless, while others are most turned on by women whose bodies are very hairy, including the legs, armpits and genital regions. Some women like their men with hairy chests, while others prefer chests as smooth and bare as a baby's.

The importance of head hair in sexual communication is a subject of continual dispute. The many stereotypes and expectations about hair length and colour are notoriously inaccurate. History, myths, even the Bible, are riddled with accounts of men with long hair, yet we are led to believe that it is principally a female sex signal.

Far left: *Dark-haired women are generally judged to be more serious and shorter hair is associated with qualities of strength.*

Left: *Long hair is regarded as particularly alluring and feminine, and changes the apparent shape of the woman's face. Blonde women are assumed to be more sexually desirable yet are judged less friendly and trustworthy.*

Above: *Red hair is stereotypically linked to a fiery, tempestuous disposition.*

Right: *Curly hair again totally changes the appearance and apparent personality as well as affecting the attractiveness of the wearer.*

Biologically this is untrue, as male and female hair grows at the same rate and to the same length. (For a full discussion on the reasons behind this erroneous stereotype, read *Femininity* by Susan Brownmiller.) Nevertheless, we cling to the fantasy that very feminine women have long hair, even though we have all seen very attractive, highly sexual women with moderately short or even very short hair. However, women with long hair do use it as a powerful part of their non-verbal sexual repertoire, as do long-haired men. Those with long hair can toss back their heads in provocative preening gestures; they can play peek-a-boo by peeking out from behind their hair like a curtain. They can run their fingers through it seductively, wrap it around their necks like a silken scarf, hide their shoulders with it, curl it sensuously around their fingers, or even pass the ends of it into their mouths and gently suck on it.

The colour of hair sends a strong signal too. Although there is no scientific evidence to support any of the hair colour stereotypes, blondes are reputed to have more fun. Blonde women are often associated with sexuality and party-loving personalities. Blond men are taken less seriously and, like red-headed men, are probably believed less. Black- and brown-haired women are often thought of as more serious; dark-haired men are traditionally assumed to be more romantic than the average and red-headed women are presumed to have tempers to match their fiery hair colour, but again these stereotypes are based on myth. Unfortunately, we may be affected by these stereotypes in such a way as to influence our self-perception as well as our perception of others.

Both the colour of hair and the way in which it frames our face affects the relative appearance of our skin tone and even the apparent colour of our eyes. Wigs are an unsatisfactory solution to a desire for an alteration in hair appearance because they are temporary disguises rather than being indicative of real change. However, they can be a good way of experimenting with possible radical changes. Hair extensions can be a useful compromise, but the most effective course of action is to have the courage to decide on a hairstyle and colour that feel absolutely right for you.

What really matters is that your hair is clean, well-groomed and in good condition. These simple things send a message of solid self-esteem and sound health and show that you think about the way your hair frames your face. Whatever your hair type or colour, try to love your hair. It is one of the first things we notice about others and it will make a big difference to you if you feel good about it. Here is a curious fact: some women report that their hair texture becomes softer when they are sexually aroused or in love.

Hair preening always accompanies sexual arousal. Men and women automatically touch their hair when they are attracted to someone, when they wish to make themselves look more sexy and when they want to communicate interest in another person. The hair stroke and hair flick are used equally by both sexes but provoke a stronger response when they are enacted by women. Of particular potency is the following gesture: the woman uses her hands to hold her hair up on top of her head, while glancing sideways and distinctly raising the shoulder that is nearest to her desired prey.

Remember not to hide your face behind your hair – your face is too important in non-verbal sexual communication to camouflage it, unless you do not want to be seen. Men who are in the presence of a woman whose hair is tied up, or tucked inside some kind of hat, should take note if she

Right: There can be few more directly sexual non-verbal communications than the signals being displayed by this woman. The combination of the raised shoulder, the tilted head, the sideways glance, the pouting lips and the phallic pen provocatively slipped into her open mouth together indicate sexual arousal and suggest that this is due to the presence of someone she finds highly attractive. This combination of sexual signals is exploited in advertising posters and commercials. It is also used by men but to a lesser degree as the effect seems to be less powerful on women.

looks in their direction as she lets it down and flicks her hair. This particular preening gesture often accompanies sexual interest in a woman.

IT'S THE WAY YOU SAY IT

It's not what you say but the way that you say it! Try saying to yourself, 'Oh darling, I love you.' Now try saying it aloud. Now say it in a heavy French accent. Now with a funny croaky voice. Now with your tongue pressed into your cheek. Now say it really slowly, making the 'Oh' last a long time. Say it really breathily this time. Now put the emphasis on 'I'. Then shift the emphasis to 'you'. Say it as if you were frightened. Say it loudly. Say it hurriedly. Try whispering it, exaggerating and punctuating each word as if it were a separate sentence. Now try rolling it off your tongue 'joined up' like one long word. Now say it rolling the 'r' in darling. Now say it insincerely. Now be very surprised. Now be really accusing as you spit it out. Then be very quiet and say it as you do when you really do love someone. You will see that musical tonality is more attractive than a voice that adheres to a monotone.

ON THE TELEPHONE

After a first meeting which has gone well you will probably have exchanged telephone numbers, though one of you may have withheld it. Social norms differ, but in the West most men ask for a girl's number first. She may offer it, or may refuse while asking for the man's instead. Business cards may also be proffered. If both numbers are exchanged then the man is generally expected to make the first contact. He may, of course, be too nervous to do so, or may mislay the piece of paper. Alternatively, the woman may take the intiative. In the event that no post-meeting call takes place, either the man or the woman may organize a social gathering a couple of weeks later and invite the other party together with several guests.

Home numbers are more intimate than work numbers, though work numbers are probably safer for a woman to hand out. Getting the telephone number of someone you want to meet again sometimes calls for some resourcefulness, such as obtaining it from mutual friends and so on. Whatever the circumstances of obtaining the number, the first telephone call is usually invigorating and even nerveracking. Telephones hide most of the subtleties of our voices because of their low-fidelity electronic reproduction. Unless both parties happen to own video-telephones, they must rely utterly on the reduced auditory non-verbal communication signals. Without the numerous visual

cues we focus on the tiniest variation of tone and speed; moods can be guessed at quite accurately just from the sound of a voice.

Doubts and hesitations are as obvious as the sound of someone smiling as they talk to you.

Given this, the best way to make a telephone call is to imagine that the person you are calling is in the room with you, that he or she can see you, so that you take conscious note of your body language and adjust it accordingly. Flirt with your prospective date by sending them attractive and inviting body signals, even though they're not actually present. They will be able to 'see' you by picking up the cues given by your voice. The advantage of the telephone is that you have time on your side to prepare your body prior to making a call. If someone phones you and you are not ready to talk to them, ask them to call again in five minutes. Do some relaxation exercises; smile, think positively, be alive and animated, work up

located in that part of the brain that is assigned to memory and other higher-thinking processes. This is why smells are capable of eliciting particularly strong memories. One woman recounted this surprising story: as a teenager she had had an obsessive love for an older man who always wore a lot

confidence. Take that five minutes to think carefully about what you actually want to say. And if it is you who is taking the plunge, stand tall and rally your own self-esteem. OK, make that call!

THE SMELL OF SEX

All of us stink! We all smell too! Our nose is a wonderfully sensitive organ. Signals from the nose are interpreted by the brain in the olfactory bulb,

of a particular aftershave lotion. Although their relationship never in fact became a physical one, she nevertheless indulged in numerous sexual fantasies centred around him. Years later she found herself shockingly attracted to a man she met at a party. She was so sexually aroused that she was in a state of near orgasm by the time she kissed him. As she rubbed her nose against his neck, she suddenly realized that her new acquaintance was wearing the same aftershave as her long-forgotten teenage love.

But do perfumes and deodorants, body creams and oils, and the many washing agents and conditioners we use on our clothes actually enhance our sexual appeal? From the vast amounts of money that is spent upon them you would think the answer must be yes, but it is not that clear.

Left: 'Eskimo kissing' can be surprisingly intimate and arousing, but it is our sense of smell that is important in understanding what makes us attractive and what attracts us to others. Pheromones are the natural scents that we all give off and they seem to have a strong effect on everyone around us. There is some evidence to suggest that our natural body scents may vary depending on our level of sexual arousal and that these changes can be detected, usually subconsciously, by other people. Some perfumes may enhance our sexual scent but the majority probably disguise it.

Obviously a memory-related attraction prompted by a particular smell is only a rare event. However, when we buy perfumes for our lovers are we saying to them, 'I wish you smelled like someone I loved before' or, worse still, 'I don't like your natural smell, so I'd like you to cover it with this, please'?

Our natural smell is unique. Each one of us has a particular odour produced by a complex combination of our skin texture and the sebaceous glands under the surface of the skin that secrete various oily deposits. Our smell depends on the level of various chemicals in our body, and on the natural sugars, acids, alkaline and salts that are deposited on the skin's surface and released from apocrine glands located in the groin, the armpits, the mouth, the eyelids, the nipples and, to a lesser degree, the backs of the knees, the wrists and the palms of the hands.

It is this personal smell that carries a great deal of important information to the olfactory centre of a potential lover. If the body smell is not right, there will almost certainly be no attraction. We therefore do ourselves a disservice by applying too many products that cover up our olfactory identity. So why do we do it? The answer is simple. Our clothes trap and hold the natural scents – pheromones – that are released from the various sites around our body (which are usually hair-covered as the hairs help distribute the scents into the air around us), causing them to become stale and unpleasant. Perhaps this is an explanation for the high incidence of holiday romances – the summer holiday allows us to spend most days and evenings largely unclothed, our pheromones wafting naturally into the air around us.

Research shows that our body smells change as we become turned on, and that the scents given off even change during love-making as we approach orgasm. In her excellent book *Body Language*, Jane Lyle describes how scientists established that a woman smells significantly different during ovulation – the time when she is most likely to become pregnant and therefore most needs to attract a mate – and that men are capable of detecting this change.

The pheromones in men and women are different. The male pheromone, called androsterone, is related to the male sex hormone testosterone, which is produced in the testes. Perfume-makers employ a chemically similar substance called andostenediol, which is added to various perfumes for men with the specific intent of increasing sexual attraction.

Androsterone is especially evident in the armpits and groin. Thus a man who is clean but not covered with a perfume, and who has not blocked up the pores of his skin with a deodorant, is most likely to sexually arouse women. This may be why men often sit with their legs open when they are trying to seduce. It is not just that they wish to show their suggestive crotch bulge – they also unconsciously want their natural scent to waft into the air. We put far too much energy and money into dehumanizing natural smells and bombarding our noses with artifical distractions.

Women's pheromones, called capulins, are released in pre-sweat glands and also vaginal secretions. The rules about cleanliness apply to women in the same way as they do to men. Women, though, are often able to identify a perfume that seems to exaggerate their natural smell. A little perfume goes a very long way: if you can smell it on yourself you've probably got too much on. Some natural scents have long been associated with sexual arousal – for example ambergris, civet, musk, vanilla and violets.

It takes courage to do it, but the most likely action to turn on a person by smell is to unbutton your shirt, rub your hand under your armpit and then wipe your face and neck with it! However, this is definitely not a technique that you should try out on a stranger.

People who smoke are at a considerable disadvantage when it comes to smelling the subtle scents of sex. Smokers cover up many of their own natural scents, too, which puts others literally 'off the scent'. Smokers therefore miss out on a principal sensory sensual pleasure.

THE GENTLE FACE OF LOVE

When we are sexually attracted to someone our face changes. Men and women both have less sagging under and around the eyes, and the muscles on the whole face generally tone up. Women's skin appears softer and more youthful: this is what is sometimes described as the 'glow' of being in love. Sexual arousal also brings a flush of colour into a woman's cheeks and a high degree of arousal may produce a blush appearing on the neck, shoulders and even chest.

Men often touch their faces more than they normally do when they catch sight of a woman whom they find attractive. They may stroke their cheeks, touch their ears, finger their neck on the front and sides, and hold their head higher and more upright. Their eyes may also appear to be brighter and more 'alive'.

Women stroke each part of their necks more, and touch their mouths and lips with their fingertips. They also hold their heads up more, and their eyes seem more sparkling. General muscle tone improves and the cheekbones seem to be more

pronounced. The eminent researcher Ray Birdwhistell estimated that the human face can produce no fewer than 250,000 expressions – an astonishing figure. Universally recognized facial expressions indicate happiness, surprise, fear, anger, sadness and disgust. But what of love, lust, passion, intense pleasure, or is it pain? And sometimes we actually cry with laughter, contorting our face in a complex map of contradictions.

Babyish faces are considered to be more attractive in women than in men. In one experiment it was shown that men judged women to be most attractive when their faces combined the immature features of wider-spaced eyes, high forehead and small chin and nose with the mature features of wide cheekbones and slim cheeks. Perhaps this combination produces the effect of vulnerability and authority – an irresistible combination for a large number of men.

Finally, when we are attracted to someone our face muscles become more animated. Try putting into practice everything you have learned about the eyes, mouth and face. Experiment with employing different facial expressions when you are at a party and see which ones elicit the most rewarding responses.

Right: Extended eye-to-eye gazing is characteristic behaviour between people who are falling in love. Sometimes people close their eyes when they are highly aroused to concentrate more on the physical sensations by excluding visdual distractions. Men tend to rely more directly on visual information for stimulation and excitement during love-making. Couples who keep their eyes open before, during and after love-making report a much greater sense of emotional connection with each other.

CHAPTER NINE

HANDING IT OUT

Our hands perform three main roles in sexual non-verbal communication. They touch, point and signal. We use our hands for a great many gestures too, to illustrate, dramatize and punctuate points in our conversation. We can draw in the air with them, imitate and animate and parody movement, and indicate when we wish to speak or when we want to invite someone else to speak to us. We can even call a crowd to silence just by touching a finger to our lips. Such is the power that lies at our fingertips.

The hands are wonderful things for launching graphic non-verbal insults and can mimic various sexual acts by their interplay. Some of these sexual gestures are very culture-specific. For example, in the Netherlands it is highly suggestive to form your hand into a clenched fist with the thumb protruding from between the knuckles of your first and middle fingers, known as the fig gesture.

POINTING

'Don't point, it's rude!' How many times were you told that as a child? Frequently, probably. It is a highly contradictory command, given that as infants we are taught the names of objects (and people) by having them pointed out to us, and as toddlers learning to speak we gain great delight from pointing at things while saying their names. But we soon learn it is impolite to point at people – it is as if a laser beam comes flying out of the end of our finger, magically affecting the pointee.

The negative connotations of pointing are thus either attacking or else accusatory, but even as adults we do like pointing at things we want. Just imagine you are feasting your eyes on a generously stocked sweet-trolley in a restaurant. You point at the most scrumptious-looking chocolate gâteau and say 'I'll have some of that, please!' Well, the same is true when it comes to sex. We love to point at the object of our

*Above: The dreaded wet fish handshake is an instant turn off, while the knuckle-crushing vice grip is equally unwelcome. Research shows that both men and women should offer a firm and confident handshake for best effect. **Right:** The claims made by palmists that the lines on our hands communicate secrets of our personality and destiny are of doubtful validity. Nevertheless, we do communicate extensively with our hand movements.*

sexual desire and at our own best assets as part of our courtship ritual. Sometimes we point with our finger in the gun position, to indicate to another that we have 'chosen' them. It is as powerful as actually throwing a line to them. We can use a pointing signal over a long distance, especially in conjunction with a smile, an eyebrow flash and a four-second eye gaze.

We also point more subtly, vaguely motioning in someone's direction, perhaps holding a glass or using our entire hand.

In conjunction with moving our arms, we can point towards someone in such a way as to invite them to join us or to indicate that we are having a conversation about them. We often point and signal simultaneously; we beckon people towards us with a sweeping motion of a cupped hand, or with just one finger hooked and moving backwards and forwards, scratching a little in the air. The precise meaning of finger, hand and arm movements changes according to which part of each we use and to which culture we belong. The acceptability of set motions and degrees of self-consciousness in executing them also vary a lot.

Often, without realizing it, we point at our genitals. This is a very sexually charged non-verbal signal and is more often performed by men. Crotch-pointing can be overt or implied. Even a hand pushed into a pocket is suggestive, as the viewer's eye is automatically drawn down the arm in search of the hand. The 'cowboy' stance can take various forms. The thumbs can be hooked into the tops of the trousers, the belt, a belt loop or the pockets (side or top depending on the cut) and anywhere from one finger to four may do the actual pointing. One or both hands on the hips can also point towards the genitals; the angle of the arms makes a big difference between masculine and feminine gesture signals.

The classic stance of the gunslinger about to draw his pistols is still used in advertising posters to sell macho products and also by male and

Above: By pointing with an apparently head-supporting hand we can draw another's gaze to ours. This gesture increases the likelihood of initiating an intimate eye exchange of extended duration, which in turn leads to increased arousal and attraction.

Right: Clean, fresh-smelling, well-cared-for hands and nails are aesthetic in men and women equally. It takes relatively little effort to make our hands attractive. Feeling good about our hands means we are less likely to hide them.

Left: Who fancies who? Complex signals create an apparent paradox. Both couples are mirroring with their arms and have eye contact. However, the man on the right has his torso and legs directed towards the woman on the left and she has her crossed leg extended forwards, pointing back at him, her foot almost touching his leg.

Below: Some time later the relationships are confirmed. The nearer couple mirror with heads, torso, arms and legs. On one side their arms form a protective barrier across the table, separating them from the other couple.

female pop stars to great effect. Madonna and Prince both point with their sexual assets, and many women recount that they love driving men wild by pointing their breasts at them or by hunching their shoulders forwards so as to increase the apparent fullness of their breasts and the depth of their cleavage.

We use our hands and fingers to point at vital sexually communicative features including our eyes and mouths. By raising a finger in the air during dialogue we immediately 'catch' the other person's eye, and can then direct that gaze where we wish.

HAND AND ARM SIGNALS

We signal our attraction with our hands in several ways. When we greet someone there is often a handshake of some description. As discussed earlier, a firm handshake is most desirable for both men and women, but a handshake any longer than five seconds will imply a desire for greater intimacy. A gentle tug can signal attraction, and even the subtlest squeeze on the fleshy part of the palm can make a person of either sex want to have you hold his or her hand.

We can signal high status or supreme confidence – although it can be dangerously near the edge of unattractive arrogance – by placing our hands behind (not on top of) the head. The finger steeple is also a sign of great confidence. If you are lucky enough to have beautiful hands and fingernails, show these off as much as possible by using plenty of hand movements when you communicate. The possession of nice hands is rated very highly among physical attributes. However, if you do not have nice hands do not hide them by sitting on them, keeping them in your pockets and so on as your hands are too vital a link in the communication chain not to employ them fully.

If you lean gently forwards as you shake hands, it will increase your mutual state of arousal and will make your intentions more clear. The unsubtle palm scratch of your opposite's hand with your middle finger is not recommended. A very fleshy 'mount of Venus', the part of the palm at the base of the thumb, is claimed by some to indicate high sensuality, and the proponents of palmistry will argue that the lines on our hands reveal a whole host of secret signals about us. True or not, asking to read someone else's palm is one of the most common and transparent excuses many newly courting couples give each other for fondling each other's hands for the first time.

suggestive and arousing. Women tend to anoint their wrists with perfume, yet men do not – a puzzling anomaly, as wrist jewellery is common to both women and men.

Often very suggestively, we use our hands to caress inanimate objects. These are usually phallic in shape and may hint at sexual acts which we may or may not be daydreaming about as we talk to someone we fancy. A dinner table provides plenty of opportunities for selecting phallic objects, ranging from the ubiquitous candle to the pieces of cutlery, the wine bottle, the stem of a wine glass,

We use our hands to signal interest in someone by moving them into another's personal space. We edge our hands forward across the surface of a table or bar. We reveal our open palms towards the person we desire as a peaceful gesture of good will. An open palm is friendly and can be very inviting. Many of the signals we send with our hands are aimed at suggesting touch.

The wrists have always been considered highly erotic, especially on women, and to this day, for reasons unknown, the display of the wrist is highly

Left: Hands and arms emphasize and animate speech and can also send signals of attraction and sexual intent. Open-palm gestures are warm and attractive. Here the man's hands are animated and pointing. It is as if a physical line were extending from the ends of his fingertips to form a wall either side of the woman, drawing her in and excluding others at the same time.

Right: A hand extended towards someone acts as a pointer in the direction of the person to whom we are attracted. In this case the hand on the table also crosses over into the woman's personal space zone. Her upward-facing open palms indicate she is relaxed and unthreatened by his advance.

Far right: The wrist display is a particularly alluring and very feminine gesture. It is often observed in smokers as they put a cigarette to their lips, though a cigarette is not a prerequisite. Exaggerated wrist displays and limp-wrist gestures are used by drag artists to emphasize their femininity.

HANDING IT OUT

the pepper grinder and many others. We can even use our hands, and especially our fingers, to mimic oral sex, sucking and licking food from them.

SHOULDERS AND ARMS

When we meet someone we like, not only do we give him or her an eyebrow flash, we also give a shoulder flash! Without realizing it, men and women shrug their shoulders when they find each other attractive. The movement is small and rapid

When we are receiving unwanted advances we tend to grip our forearms with our hands and tense our shoulders, hug ourselves around the waist, or partially protect ourselves with one arm across our body, touching the opposite side shoulder or the neck. If someone adopts a defensive position such as this in response to an approach from you, take the message and change your behaviour. Smile more and try giving the person extra room. Change your posture and position in relation to them and try motivating removal of the block by offering a hand to shake, or a glass to

but if you notice that the person facing you does it, you know they are attracted to you, perhaps even before they are aware of it themselves.

The hands and arms can also signal negative feelings about someone coming on to us. It is possible to indicate disinterest by building a blockade with our arms or hands. We can literally shut someone out by covering our eyes with our hands, or closing our eyes for a prolonged length of time. We can block our body protectively by folding our arms fully, with our fists clenched or flat.

hold. Once the barrier is down, use positive non-hostile non-verbal signalling and see if it stays down. If it does, your presence is no longer being completely rejected.

People also cross their arms because they are cold, because they are shy, because they have got a stiff neck or aching back, or because they might be busy thinking about something internal and are not necessarily rejecting you at all.

You should know, however, that crossing your arms reduces your overall sensory intake. It really does create a shield. If, for example, you watch a film with your arms folded you will remember less of the film than if you had sat with an open body position! You may habitually be shutting out a good deal of the potential pleasure in life just by crossing your arms. Check how often you do, and try unfolding your arms to feel what a difference it makes. Since most parliaments of the world are now televised, politicians have much to learn about this. When a politician is giving a speech his confederates should all sit with their arms uncrossed, while his opposers should fold their arms. At present, many political leaders appear to be surrounded by colleagues who do not wish to listen to them!

TOUCH

Touch. Even the word alone sounds sexy. Every square inch of your body is sensitive to touch. Some parts of ourselves we touch in public, at random and with impunity: our hair, hands, forearms, necks, faces. Other skin surfaces we stroke or rub when in a particular mood: our foreheads when we are thinking; the lower back when we are stressed; the stomach when we are anxious. Our erogenous zones and sexual skin surfaces we deliberately touch or rub when in private, to wash or to arouse ourselves. But sexual self-touch also takes place in public, and is an integral part of courtship behaviour.

Preening is a way of flattering ourselves and flirting with others simultaneously. It occurs throughout the animal kingdom, with, usually, the males of the species parading to impress potential mates. Both men and women preen themselves alone, often as part of the dressing to go out ritual. Once in the presence of the opposite sex, they begin to preen again. The most common preening

gestures are touching the hair with hands, comb or brush; touching the face (normally with fingertips) in brief stroking gestures, including wiping the eyebrows, touching the lips, stroking the cheeks, and smoothing the beard or moustache.

Out on the town keen preeners glance at their reflections whenever they get the chance. Women frequently check their make-up, and young teenage males glance anxiously at mirrors to check how the red spot they squeezed an hour earlier is doing.

If we want to send non-verbal sexual signals to another person we do put on a display by preening in that direction, flicking our hair back from our face, for example, and running a hand through it while simultaneously casting a glance towards our target. We brush imaginary fluff from our shoulders, pick at invisible specks of dust on our clothes and endlessly rearrange our whole attire, rubbing our hands over the surface of the material, smoothing ruffles, pulling at cuffs, readjusting and tucking-up neck scarves or ties and so on.

If the clothes we are wearing are made from fine, sensuous materials – especially silks, suede and fine cottons – we may arouse ourselves with their touch against our skin. By rubbing our hands up and down our clothes or our skin we may also be mimicking what we hope we will be able to do to another person, or we might be showing them where we would like to be touched. Without realizing it, we are also turning ourselves on.

We tend to stroke our wrists and hands against our forearms, particularly if bare-skinned, and then touch the outside of our upper thighs. If we are very turned on we may even stroke them on the inside. Women put their hands into back pockets of trousers and between their legs more often than do men. They can squeeze a hand comfortingly between folded legs and, if wearing trousers, may sit with their legs open but with a hand dropped between their legs acting as a modest fig leaf.

Women tend to stroke their breasts – especially the upper part of the breast – with a finger or with unconscious strokes of the hand. This touching may cause their nipples to become firm and erect. Although erect nipples can also be the result of temperature change or just friction against material and need not be related in any way to sexual arousal, the non-verbal signal sent by such a manifestation is sensational. Men tend to be unable to look anywhere else if they notice a woman's erect nipples beneath clothing – which they invariably will.

Auto-erotic signalling, as this self-touch display and preening behaviour is sometimes called, is a precursor to the touching of another person. This pre-touch stage is the 'readiness' part of pre-sexual interaction. We are preparing ourselves mentally and physically for a possible sexual encounter. Once we are ready, we demonstrate our readiness for others to see. This explains the often unnecessary self-preening we do in public. This knowledge may be used to recognize potential partners and you can even employ additional preening gestures yourself for the benefit of someone watching you. It will broadcast the non-verbal message, 'I'm doing this for me and maybe for you too. . .'

Above and left: Private preparation rituals and public preening displays are observed in both men and women during all stages of developing courtship. When we are attracted to someone we unconsciously fuss over our appearance, as if readjusting our 'mating plumage'. We tug on cuffs, readjust ties, scarves and clothes, brush away imaginary fluff from our clothes, check make up, smooth our eyebrows and touch and stroke our hair.

TOUCHING EACH OTHER

Touching is so important. It makes for a dramatic escalation of emotional intimacy in a relationship, while to touch someone is to move physically beyond their intimate space zone barrier. To invite touch is to make yourself accessible and vulnerable. This takes trust and courage and suggests that attraction is growing between you.

We have all experienced the inevitable anxieties of potential rejection. It is a nerve-racking thing to ask another person for a first date, or for a dance, or even just to strike up a conversation with them. To offer someone a hand literally, or metaphorically, and have it refused can be a substantial blow to the ego. The successful use of touch, therefore, depends on good timing and the accurate reading of the other person's non-verbal sexual signals.

The first intimate touch is usually hand to hand. This is not the formal handshake, but often a brief, apparently accidental touch, perhaps of the backs of the hands against each other. For example, if you are walking beside someone, your hand swinging by your side, it may occasionally brush your partner's. Such touches may or may not be commented on by either of you but ideally you do not apologize for touching. These accidental touches are quite safe as there is little loss of face if the other person does not reciprocate, or even if she or he physically withdraws from you.

Above: A couple on their first date are always nervous of the first overt touch and getting the timing right can be quite difficult. As a result they may begin by brushing against eachother accidentally on purpose which makes the step to deliberate touching that much easier. Walking side by side, this couple are already within the intimate space zone.

Right: They are walking so close that every so often the backs of their hands touch for a moment. What happens next is crucial. If either person wishes they can withdraw their hand to another position ensuring no further touching occurs. Otherwise they can ensure the touch is repeated. This often leads to holding hands.

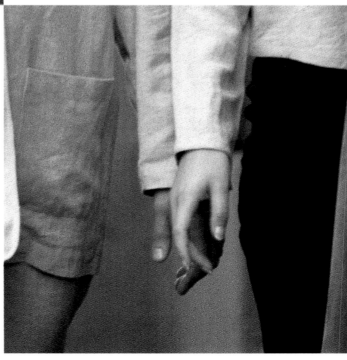

Traditionally it is men who always try to touch first but this is largely a reflection of sexist stereotypes of men being responsible for making the first move. Women are just as capable of initiating

touch but run the risk of being thought of as over-assertive, pushy, 'easy' or not playing by the rules of the game, which is especially hard on people who are just very warm and 'huggy'. 'Redraw the rules,' you might shout, but you should be aware that to initiate touch is also to send some of the first 'I'm keen on you' signals. If you are a woman who does not want to rush or be rushed, perhaps the compromise is to take deliberate active control from a passive position: you place your hands strategically so as to make them available for touch. Then the man you desire may think he has initiated a caress, thus keeping pride intact while it is actually you who guides events along.

How and when you first touch obviously depends on your situation. If you are going to rush across a busy road together you may instinctively join hands as you step off the kerb. If you are walking along side by side, you may offer your hand passively and find it being held. You may suddenly want to point out something in a shop window and grab your companion enthusiastically. Alternatively, you may guide him or her with a gentle hand on the lower back.

Above: As intimacy increases and attraction levels rise, courting couples touch each other with increasing frequency. These touches can be momentary, as with joking little slaps or pushes used during animated speech, or more sensuous strokes of the arms, face or hair. A hand placed on the back of the other person can be used to guide them or draw them closer.

Right: He wraps his hands around her and pulls her into an intimate position, but she feels ensnared and instantly pushes him away. Such misunderstandings are best avoided by sensitivity to the other person's early warning signals of discomfort. As he moved his arm into position she would have indicated her displeasure. He should have backed off sooner to avoid the embarrassment of an unpleasant confrontation.

Parties are ideal venues for first physical contact, allowing people to touch by dancing together, fast or slowly. Dancing accelerates the normal

Above and right: *Romantic encounters escalate via a series of increasingly intimate touch rituals. Deviation from the normal sequence of advances can cause annoyance and anxiety. The body language of both couples shows mutual attraction is established and acknowledged. Her hand clasped to his pointing knee, her smile and her hair preening are all indicators of a developing intimacy. The other woman's leg position and her hand on the man's hip while one of his hands touches her forearm, the other her hair, suggest that kissing will follow soon.*

progressive stages of acceptable touch. Party games such as 'sardines' are specifically designed to break the taboos of close body contact out of the normal sequence. This is what makes them exciting.

The simple act of passing any object to a person presents you with the chance to touch or be touched, whether you are handing over a pen, offering someone a light for a cigarette, or helping a woman as she puts on her coat.

Even one brief touch has a profound effect on the way we feel towards someone. In one study, psychologists rigged several everyday encounters so that subjects were touched briefly during an encounter. In one test group, students returning books to a library were touched while people in another test group were left untouched. All the subjects were then asked about their experiences at the library and their dealings with the librarian who had served them. Without exception, those who had been touched expressed warmer, more positive feelings about the experience and the staff they had interacted with. Yet they had only been lightly and briefly touched on the forearm or hand. Other research reports that waiters and waitresses who touch their customers are likely to be given larger gratuities.

A sincere sign of attraction is to preen or groom someone else. This can be done without putting on pressure or suggesting you are making assumptions about the progress of the relationship. To pluck a piece of fluff from another's lapel is completely innocuous yet bodes great potential for intimacy.

When you are engaged in a non-verbal dialogue with someone, keep reading their signs to check for invitations or acceptance of touch. If you do touch, check both your own responses and theirs. If you both feel comfortable and 'right', then continue. If the other person withdraws or tenses up, or if the non-verbal signals change abruptly, respond by releasing your hold on them and by giving them some space. Do not sulk and do not conclude that you have completely blown your chances. Keep your body language warm and positive but be aware of how much personal space your opposite needs in order to feel safe. What you want to avoid is the negative cascade of awkward feelings and misunderstandings.

A useful tip for remembering the name of someone you have just met, and for making a positive impression, is to repeat the name while simultaneously touching the back of the person's hand or forearm. If you are shaking hands you can bring your other arm forward during the handshake and just lightly tap the new acquaintance. In the next five minutes or so make a point of using the person's name in conversation and, if you can, touch him or her as you say it. The psychologist Dr David Lewis calls this 'anchoring': it creates a positive feeling in other people, connecting them to you physically and you to them. It gives you added status – you hold the authority and self-confidence to reach out and touch – and implies that you trust this person enough, and therefore like him or her enough, to risk touching. The really important point is that by moving into another person's intimate personal space you are bringing him or her into yours too.

Placing an arm around someone's waist is a very intimate act. If you time it right, it will be accepted and enjoyed. Time it wrong and you may create tension or even provoke rejection. When someone is ready for you to put your arm around his or her waist or shoulder, he or she will stand so close to you that your hips will brush together. Your arms will no longer have room to swing, and instead will hang awkwardly, knocking against each other. This is the moment to move, especially if the other person has turned his or her torso slightly towards you. For the most pleasing result, place your hand on the lower part of his or her back. With a firm hand you will make someone feel supported while allowing the warmth from your hand to stroke one of the two comfort zones of the body (the other is the stomach). This is soothing and sensual.

Touch is a precious thing, so take care not to abuse it. Being too 'touchy' with someone too soon, or with someone who is less tactile, will only lead to discomfort, rejection and perhaps to a breakdown in communication and of goodwill. Never assume that holding hands automatically entitles you to touch anywhere else. Try to remind yourself that the deliberate suspension of instant personal gratification is one of the greatest gifts you can ever grant yourself. Anticipation is the most delicious of the myriad foreplays at your disposal.

TOUCHING EACH OTHER

Here is a list of the usual sequence of touching escalation:

a) Hand to hand
b) Hand to forearm
c) Linked arms
d) Hand to shoulder
e) Arm around waist
f) Hand to hair/head
g) Lips to lips
h) Hand to neck, back, knees, breasts, thighs
i) Deep kissing
j) Hand to genitals (still clothed)
k) Mouth to breast/chest
l) Mouth to whole body
m) Hands remove each other's clothes
n) Full love-making

CHAPTER TEN

THE SEXY TORSO

Many of us misuse our bodies a lot of the time. We slouch, we slump, we let ourselves become unfit. We wear shoes designed for pixies' feet and crush our toes as we walk. We sit in chairs apparently designed to distort our backs, carry loads that tear our muscles, and so on – the list of self-inflicted tortures is depressingly long. Our physical posture can mirror our moods. A 'depressed' stance can make us feel

slightly depressed. Equally, feelings of depression can cause our body to adopt a 'depressed' attitude. When we are feeling positive our posture tends to be positive and, by the same token, a confident posture tends to make us feel good.

When you are next at a crowded beach or a swimming pool, notice what happens when a man and a woman walk towards each other, look each other up and down, and walk on. As the two approach they both draw in their stomach muscles to make the muscles appear highly toned. This is particularly significant considering that, of all the muscles that affect male sexual performance during coitus, it is the stomach muscles that matter most. In order to be fit for fine and long-lasting love-making, strengthen your stomach muscles. Do sit-ups and leg-lifts, enrol in exercise classes – anything that will improve the stomach strength.

At the same time as pulling in our gut to impress a sexual prospect we puff up the chest. Women have the advantage of breasts with which they can emphasize this change of posture. As a woman becomes sexually aroused her breasts and nipples swell, making the latter appear redder; the muscle tone increases and the breasts slightly elevate. A salvo of sexual signals like this catches men broadside.

In a correct posture we hold our heads erect and maximize our height. Our faces take on a generally more youthful appearance. The bags and folds around the eyes

Above and right: Dancers make perfection of movement and posture look so easy, but their grace is the consequence of tortuous training. Our posture creates an instant impression. Extremes are equally undesirable: a ramrod-straight, stiff back and awkward stance is as unattractive as a slumped one. You do not have to be a trained dancer to look relaxed and comfortable yet poised and graceful.

are reduced, the creases on the brow are smoothed and the eyes are brightened. It is as if we are programmed to send the non-verbal signal, 'I am a potential mate. I am fit, young, strong, healthy and my muscles are toned up and primed for sex. See for yourself.'

Once two people have walked past each other they tend to allow themselves to deflate rapidly back to their original posture. However, someone with a generally well-balanced, upright posture really stands out as special and attractive. Such a person has presence, and will be described as elegant, distinguished and beautiful.

The condition and posture of our torso sends a clear subliminal message to interested parties about our readiness to reproduce. This may sound somewhat primitive, but it is after all what underlies all the complex rituals that surround non-verbal sexual communication.

Be body-aware. When you are exchanging non-verbal signals check that you are keeping your body as well-presented as possible, but not stiff. Whatever the positioning and movement of your body, ask yourself how you would look as a sculpture if you were to freeze at any particular instant. Allow your body to be comfortable. This will make a great difference to your own self-esteem and to how sexy you are judged to be.

As you begin to converse with someone, turn your torso towards him or her. If he or she mirrors your movement, the stakes of the encounter are being raised. The closer you bring the central part of your body to his or hers, the more your intimate zones barriers will begin to merge. Each of us carries an invisible field of energy around us and it can be very exciting and arousing to bring two of these fields together.

THE BACK

Our backs are beautiful, but we sometimes forget all about them. The dictates of fashion mean that women have a considerable advantage over men here. An expanse of back, or even glimpses of it through translucent material or peek-a-boo gaps in

the cloth, send a fabulous sexual signal. But how do you make it clear who you are showing your back to? You have a choice of tactics at your disposal: you can either establish eye contact facing the person you like and then turn around to show

them your back, or, more powerfully, turn your back to them but slant a glance back over your shoulder towards them.

The shoulders are eminently capable of flashing sexual signals. A shoulder revealed, stroked or shrugged can be deliciously provocative. The curves and roundness of shoulders, particularly in women, are sensuous and arousing — as long as they are not slouching.

MOVING TO THE MUSIC

You may have observed the way in which people of high status tend to keep their torsos relatively still, letting their faces, arms and hands do all the signalling that bring a dialogue to life. The exception to this rule is in places where music is playing. We all know that music really can be the food of love. The elixir that changes our moods, it

114

conveys those sentiments which can be hard to put into words and, more important still, it animates the rhythm in our bodies.

To be a skilled lover requires some degree of talent for rhythm. It is something we look for in prospective partners, and we can see it most obviously in the way a person moves their body in response to a beat.

In most cultures of the world, both music and dance are central components of courtship rituals.

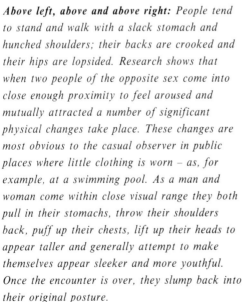

Above left, above and above right: People tend to stand and walk with a slack stomach and hunched shoulders; their backs are crooked and their hips are lopsided. Research shows that when two people of the opposite sex come into close enough proximity to feel aroused and mutually attracted a number of significant physical changes take place. These changes are most obvious to the casual observer in public places where little clothing is worn – as, for example, at a swimming pool. As a man and woman come within close visual range they both pull in their stomachs, throw their shoulders back, puff up their chests, lift up their heads to appear taller and generally attempt to make themselves appear sleeker and more youthful. Once the encounter is over, they slump back into their original posture.

Sustained external rhythms such as drumming can change your internal rhythms: your metabolic and heart rates, your breathing and your arousal level. Rhythms can even send you into states of trance, as with the whirling dervish dancers, or in the frenetic, ecstatic and euphoric moods experienced by head bangers and, more recently, ravers.

The melodies and harmonies of music can cause rushes of emotion to sweep through the body. Music is so powerful a medium of non-verbal communication that it can set the whole tone of an encounter: exciting and manic, classical and calm, soothing and New Age, romantic and sentimental. A shared liking of similar kinds of music often provides valuable common ground when two potential lovers meet and provides a happy and enjoyable way of going on to increased intimacy.

One very erotic dance or pre-dance movement a woman can make is to swing or gyrate her hips while standing still, with or without hands on hips. Armpits can be flashed while dancing, with the hands raised in the air or touching the hair, providing a provocative sensual signal. The same is true of rolling shoulders and running one's hands over one's body.

Dancing is a dramatic way for us to put on a preening display for prospective mates. We generally have full social permission to strut our stuff, and it is an acceptable way of showing off our talents. Many dance movements involve the swaying of hips and torso and the stylized mimicking of sexual acts. The dance floor provides ample opportunity to observe the body language of others: the way we dance reflects our mood, shows how vividly we respond to music and gives onlookers strong clues about our personality. Our body movements will certainly show if we like the music we are dancing to. On the dance floor, the mirroring or postural echo phenomenon can be employed to great effect. You can dance in synchrony with someone you have never even spoken to. This dance language will quickly tell you if the other is attracted to you. If she or he begins to mirror your dance movements this is a positive signal; conversely, if your dance partner changes movement every time you begin to mirror him or her, then take the hint and withdraw gracefully.

The dominance of pop music, from its beginnings in the 1950s right up to today's techno and rave music, has meant that successive generations have broken away from formalized dance steps to styles of dancing that can be done solo. This does not mean that sexual body language is practised any less now than in the past – it has simply changed. Dance has become an expression of the independent self and the expectation of dancing 'with' another person is gone. Contemporary Western discotheques are not just venues for potential partners to meet and dance – they also allow single people to express themselves with all the richness of body language they choose. Consequently, dance remains a headily potent means of non-verbal sexual communication.

When groups of men and women gather at dance venues they exhibit certain stereotyped behaviours. The women dance in a group together, sometimes forming a circle, which apparently excludes men. Men, in contrast, tend to gather in groups at the edge of the dance floor, or to prowl around in packs like wolves on the hunt. If the men dance it is normally in pairs or alone, and they take their cue from the dance floor, when they notice possibly single girls dancing outside the female circle.

People not dancing but wanting to do so will indicate this with their bodies. Although they may

Right: The male chest and the female breasts have both long been celebrated as central features of physical attraction and important tools in sexual non-verbal communication – yet the much-neglected back, in both men and women, is also a very sexy part of the body that can be displayed as part of the courting ritual. Its skin is wonderfully sensitive and is an often neglected erogenous zone. A bare back is, however, quite vulnerable, as unlike the front it cannot be protected by the arms, and it takes a good deal of nerve to wear clothing that reveals as much as the dress shown here.

be talking to others, they will move their hands or feet gently to the rhythm of the music, or sway their upper torso and shoulders in small dance movements. If you are interested in asking someone to dance, wait to see these 'I wish I were dancing' body signals before moving in. The more obvious the movements the more likely it is that a person will accept. Also watch for an alteration in body language as the music changes. If someone is not dancing it may be because the track playing does not appeal. If he or she suddenly becomes more animated facially, beats the rhythm more vigorously or even 'dances' sitting down, you can be pretty sure that the tune just starting has a strong appeal, and your invitation to dance is more likely to be accepted.

Part of the dance routine will include the stroking of the waistline – especially in women, as this emphasizes the width of the hips and draws attention to the feminine body shape, which in its own right is one of the principal non-verbal sexual signals, expressing the gender at a glance. Men also stroke their waistline to emphasize the stomach muscles and to contrast this area with their wider shoulders and larger chests – the masculine gender shape signal.

The slow dance is often the first opportunity we have to become really intimate with someone. How we respond while we are engaged upon it tells us everything we need to know about our levels of sexual readiness: where we place our arms; how we move our bodies; how close together we bring our upper torsos; how much we allow our leg or knee to project between the legs of the other person; how tightly we hold each other; how much we relax into each other's arms; the amount of time we spend looking into each other's eyes; whether our partner is looking over our shoulder or resisting our attempts to move his or her face into position so that kissing is possible; all these signals are to be looked out for.

The way we angle the torso towards or away from a person also sends a clear message of purpose. A full torso-to-full torso position is quite hostile unless we are dancing, which not only allows us to adopt this pose within social conventions but also ensures

that any confrontational stance is not maintained for long – the end of a particular tune provides a convenient opportunity to withdraw gracefully from any further intimacy with no excuses needed. Orientation is most seductive, when we approach from the side to form two sides of a triangle, with the arm or leg of one or both completing the third side so as to exclude anyone else from our interaction.

You will by now have realized the vital importance of the torso in sexual non-verbal communication: the way we hold our body, the degree of personal comfort we display, the angle of our body, the muscle tone and the shape of our abdomen, the degreee of exposure of our backs and chests – all these factors contribute to the impression we make upon our potential partners, long before we are close enough for eye contact to be made.

FANCY LEGWORK

The legs have their own sexual language, and are particularly involved in the blocking and territory-marking aspects of seduction. Endless myths surround the sexual signals of legs. For example, many people think that crossing the legs is a defensive signal or a way of repressing sexuality. Sometimes this may be the case, but legs that cross can send many other signals to interested onlookers too.

The leg-twine is the most potent yet polite sexual signal a woman can send with her legs and is a particularly attractive pose when viewed from front on. The legs are crossed in such a way as to appear highly toned, with the length of the upper leg pressed against the lower leg and the uppermost foot often pointing towards the ground. This is a classically feminine leg pose and is less attractive when done by men. Women also have the ability to double twist their legs, which can be very sexual but is also associated with feeling anxious or pent up like a coiled spring.

The standard leg-cross, where the right leg is rested over the left in a relaxed manner, can be used as a protective or closed position, depending on the context. A protective stance is adopted when the leg-crosser feels threatened – the crotch area is hidden behind the shield of the upper thighs pressed together.

If legs are crossed defensively this will usually be accompanied by a range of other defensive signals – the arms may well be folded, eye contact will be furtive rather than flirtatious, a handbag may be strategically placed on the lap as a large fig-leaf substitute and the torso will lean away from the accompanying person, or lean forwards with the head supported by a shielding arm.

Legs that are crossed as a way of pointing send out a vital signal. When seated we tend to cross our legs towards a person we are attracted to, and away from someone

Above and right: Long, well-toned legs are considered very attractive in both men and women. The appeal seems to be less to do with height than with the apparent length of the legs relative to the rest of the body, while good muscle tone is sexually attractive because it replicates the bodily changes that occur during sexual arousal.

to whom we wish to send a negative sexual signal. We can point a crossed leg directly at someone we fancy, or in their general direction. We also point with our feet and especially the toes.

We point with our feet when we stand up, too. We point a foot towards someone who attracts us, or move a leg towards them. We can shift our weight onto the back leg with the other leg forwards and bent at the knee. The female knee has a particularly erotic effect on some men, its roundness hinting at the shape of breast and buttock. The spread buttocks of the female are the principal mating invitation posture, and this can be mimicked by drawing both knees up into a provocative teasing posture.

We can point with our knees too, and if we really stretch a leg towards someone we can use it as an invitation to follow it back to where it begins. Men tend to use the standard leg cross through habit or simply because they sit in a bad posture. They may feel that it eases muscle pain or tension in the back, but although crossing the legs may sometimes relieve pain it is in fact not good for the posture.

Both men and women sometimes cross their legs at the ankle, and the message this gives should be interpreted in the context of accompanying signals – particularly how widely apart the legs are spread. Legs parted in a great yawning splay send a crude primitive sexual signal. Nevertheless, both men and women do automatically open their legs to varying degrees when in the presence of someone they find particularly attractive. It is more common for men to sit with their legs open, often giving a crotch display, though women wearing trousers do this too. Tight-fitting trousers or leggings are highly provocative if they outline the shape of the female genitals through the material as well as emphasizing the curves of the bottom.

The cross-legged position 'open 4', where one ankle is placed atop the knee of the other leg, can be very inviting when used by either men or women, but if the hand is brought down to block the crossed leg at the angle this should be interpreted as more defensive. Women can use the leg cross to devastating effect to play peek-a-boo with

Right: The legs and feet are central indicators of sexual attraction. We often forget to pay attention to our feet because they are at the periphery of our conscious attention span: we are so busy concentrating on our facial expressions and hand and arm movements that our feet and legs can leak out our true feelings about other people. In this scene the man on the right is sitting in the standard leg-cross position but his left foot is pointing towards the standing woman. Together with his pointing hand gesture, this indicates his dialogue is directed at the standing woman, who responds by turning her face and upper torso towards him despite the fact that her leg positions clearly indicate her attachment to the other man. Meanwhile the seated woman's crossed leg, in the leg-twine position, suggests that she is attracted towards the man on her left.

men. Skirts with splits allow women crossing their legs to flash tantalizing glimpses of that which is hidden under the material. Short skirts may be worn to deliberately reveal stocking tops or suspenders, which are considered highly provocative by most men in the West.

Some folk dances incorporate courting rituals that use clothing to tantalize. For example, Spanish flamenco dancers sometimes have the hem of their skirt looped around one of their wrists so they can lift and lower the skirt as they dance. Skirts used to their full leg-revealing potential, such as those made to rise up by swirling in a circle, can allow the sexually communicative woman to pre-empt all other forms of social intercourse.

SEXY BUTTOCKS

The female curves can be emphasized by placing a hand on one or both hips and also by placing the body weight on one side, while turning the torso at an angle to the man desired. Despite humans'

ability to make love face to face, the primitive rear-entry position is still ingrained in the male psyche as the natural first position for sexual intercourse. As a result, female buttocks are a very strong source of sexual signals. Clothes that either hint at, or actually show the shape of, a woman's rear send shock waves of arousal through men. When a woman places her hand in the back pocket of a tight-fitting pair of jeans the rounded shape of the buttocks is emphasized still further. Rubbing a hand over the outline has much the same effect, a ploy that is used quite shamelessly by performers such as Madonna.

The more rounded and pert a woman's buttocks are, the stronger the sexual signal. The emphasis that so many clothes give to the breast cleavage is intended to suggest the image of swollen buttocks associated with mating behaviour. Women also visually assess the buttocks of men whenever the opportunity to do so presents itself. A small, tightly muscled behind is considered particularly sexy by most Western women.

SWINGING HIPS

Anatomical differences are responsible for the characteristic ways in which men and women walk. In women there is a greater rolling action of

forward, the barrier becomes a tactile bridge that unites them both visually and physically.

As discussed in the chapter on first impressions, our shoes say a lot about us, and how we use them can indicate our sexual mood. Sometimes a

the pelvis, which causes more swinging of the hips. This hip-swinging walk can send a powerful sexual signal. The way a woman walks across a room can mean the difference between attracting a great deal of attention and being totally ignored. Length of leg, as we saw earlier, is another arousal signal. Actual length is not as important as relative length: this is why slender legs are considered more aesthetically pleasing, as they appear to be longer. High heels increase leg length and are consequently considered sexy.

When we touch our legs and thighs or stroke our knees we send out yet another secret sexual signal, and this is particularly strong when coming from a woman. As he feels increasingly attracted, a man pushes his hips slightly forwards and stands with his feet further apart, with one foot pointing towards the woman he likes.

Either party in this sex-oriented face-off who wishes to exclude other people can extend a leg forwards in order to build a barrier. If the other party meets him or her halfway in this maneouvre with either a foot or an intertwined leg slipped

woman will slip her foot in and out of a shoe or dangle the shoe from the tip of her toes provocatively. There are enormous individual differences in taste and in what turns people on – what matters is that you wear shoes that give you confidence and feel comfortable. Don't be tempted into being a foot fashion victim.

PLAYING FOOTSIE

Playing footsie is usually, but not always, reserved for people already in a relationship. It can be very exciting, especially if it occurs out of sight (under a table, for instance) and especially if it is performed conspiratorially in the presence of others. What dinner-table entertainment could be more arousing than to have your partner (or perhaps a new acquaintance with whom you have been exchanging signals of mutual attraction) touch your feet, ankles or lower leg furtively while above the table he or she remains apparently deep in conversation with someone else, seeming to ignore

Left: It is often assumed that someone crosses their legs to create a defensive barrier. This is not necessarily so: here, although the man's leg is crossed away from the woman, the pair are in fact mirroring with both their legs and arms, and she has adopted the leg-twine position. The high degree of synchronicity in their body language suggests mutual attraction.

Below: The leg twine is especially attractive when displayed by women. The interaction between hands and legs can also be very alluring. Both men and women stroke their legs unconsciously when they are aroused, probably because the skin is more sensitive to touch.

Right: Many communication misunderstandings occur because subtle signals indicating that an intimate relationship already exists between two people are overlooked. Try to identify any hidden signals, like a gentle nudge from a foot under a table, that might link the person you are interested in to someone else.

what is going on down under. Men should beware of initiating footsie too strongly. It is better to position a foot close to one of the woman's, thereby creating the opportunity for her to accept the tip-toed invitation if she so chooses.

So the legs and feet are capable of transmitting many secret sexual signals. As with all the other signs described in this book, the language of the legs should be read along with other body signals and in the context of a particular situation. Meeting a new person of the opposite sex can be as confusing and frightening as it can be arousing and challenging. We are frequently confronted by conflicting messages, and may feel ourselves hanging in the balance, waiting to approach some-one and yet simultaneously wanting to avoid them. Relationships bring us the potential for changes of enormous importance. Even single encounters have been known to alter the course of people's lives completely.

How then do we read the complex and often contradictory non-verbal language of the whole body? The final chapter will enable you to amal-gamate the multifarious body language facts described throughout the book, to test your skills at reading signals of attraction and to realize your sexual appeal to the full.

CHAPTER TWELVE

THE WHOLE PICTURE

By now you will have learned many of the individual traits of behaviour that indicate whether sexual attraction is present or not. But just how sure can you be that someone is making a play for you? Is it just by chance that their body language seems to be saying, 'I want you'? This final chapter presents you with the chance to test your own skills at reading other people's sexual signals of attraction and explains how to interpret the often complex and sometimes contradictory signals that people display without being aware of their import.

THE RULE OF FOUR

The Rule of Four states that, 'To be sure that another person is communicating unequivocal non-verbal sexual interest in you, he or she must be displaying a minimum of four separate positive signals simultaneously, and these signals must be directed at you.'

A person who is sexually aroused may display some positive signals unconsciously, independent of other people present. Do not assume that the person displaying four signals is necessarily directing these signals at you. Also, one of the complex games that people play is to flirt with everyone except the person in whom they are really interested. You may fall victim to being used as a mere pawn in an intrigue-filled chess game.

Remember, too, that moods, feelings and physical levels of arousal can all change over short spaces of time. The ability to direct change in others and to command changes in oneself is a powerful skill well worth developing. It is also a basic human right for us to change our minds. Someone may come onto you strongly with four sexual signals, but the moment you start talking verbally to them, they may change their minds and their body language. Keep your eyes working in conjunction with your brain. Remember what you have learned to do when you receive negative

Above and right: During early courting stages couples tend to spend hours gazing at and touching each other, but it is not possible to keep up this level of mutual attention. One way of protecting a relationship during the inevitable transition stage is for both people to pay ongoing conscious notice of each other's sexual body language and to respond to the signals in a manner that maintains a spirit of their original intense love.

124

signals. There is no need to make a fool of yourself, or to make someone else feel awkward – just back off if the person has had a change of mind. Psychologists call these non-verbal negative signals de-courting signals. De-courting is most obvious through the withdrawal of attentiveness and attractiveness (attractiveness in this case is feeling that another person has a compellingly positive effect upon us) and a general reduction in rapport.

Do remember that one positive signal can lead to two, three or ten signals in five minutes, an hour or even three months. There is no limit to the length of time that may elapse between the first minutes of meeting and eventual commitment to some form of relationship. Many signals of attraction may be seen in people who are just friends. Indeed, some of the best sexual relationships develop from friendships. Test yourself. Have a look at

Left: How do you read these conflicting signals? That the man is interested in the woman is clear from his inclined head, his torso alignment, his hand in his pocket pointing at his genitals, his upright posture and the position of his feet. The woman's response is less clear. Although she is not facing her body towards him and her arms appear to be in a defensive position, there is some degree of mirroring present. Her smiling face turned to him over a raised shoulder is also very attractive and inviting.

Right: Some time later she is signalling a desire to cut off all communication. Everything about her posture indicates discomfort and defence. In contrast he is apparently still attempting to make advances to her.

the photographs on these two pages and imagine you are observing a person of the opposite sex and that he or she is aware that you are watching. How many different signals can you read?

We are dynamic creatures, labyrinthine of mind, subtle of limb, and effervescent of libido! Use your knowledge of sexual semaphore to guide a person from flashing you mixed messages to confirming his or her interest, or lack of it. You will know where you stand and how you stand to gain.

Begin by checking your own non-verbal sexual signals. Perhaps you are sending mixed messages yourself and the prospect is mirroring you. Check your own motives: if you are about to play a game with someone, ask yourself why? Will any good come from it? Will anyone get hurt? Consider changing tactics in the light of this self-analysis.

If the person in question is leaning towards you and smiling, but scanning the room for someone else, they are probably being friendly while waiting for their date. If the arms are folded but you are getting wonderful eye contact, genuine smiles, and a leg and foot being pointed at you, try handing

TIME TO TALK

There comes a point where verbal communication must begin if an encounter is to move on to the next step. If you are unsure about the signals you have been receiving, now is the time to check them out. Verbal and non-verbal dialogue interact and all the non-verbal sexual signals identified so far continue after verbal dialogue has begun.

over a drink or some object to see if they open their body up to you. If you notice face touches, hair preening and sideways glances, but the person has their legs crossed away from you and is hand in hand with someone else, they may be flirting with you even though they seem committed. On the other hand, if your non-verbal conversation skills serve you well, the commitment might be broken and they may turn their attention to you.

When a person's verbal language contradicts what their body language is saying, give greater weight to the latter. If someone tells you they are 'not interested' in a teasing and flirtatious way but continues to send you very sexual signals, they may just be playing 'hard to get' or 'chase me'. But if someone clearly means 'no, leave me alone', you must respect this. Persistence in the face of rejection seldom brings about a positive outcome.

127

Remind yourself to read the whole picture, not just a part of it. The human body speaks from head to toe. It is your self-assigned task to gather up all the different pieces of the situational jigsaw puzzle and play the detective so that you can assemble the whole puzzle correctly.

many other accompanying negative ones. The combined message may be profoundly and often disappointingly different from its individual components. Sensitive assessment of the whole picture will ultimately help you to arrive at the correct interpretation and avoid overplaying your hand.

This is easier said than done. It is all very well being able to read one or two non-verbal messages from a person's body and face, but in the real world we have to deal with numerous messages that are being sent simultaneously.

It is unwise to focus on one or two very positive non-verbal sexual signals while overlooking

CONTRADICTION

As with so many other areas of human behaviour, we are daily confronted with contradiction and inconsistency in non-verbal communication. It is a general feature of the human condition that few things are ever clear-cut. We are complex creatures who operate on many levels; a woman may be very attracted to a man at first glance but may quash her natural inclinations and desires as she remembers that she is already committed elsewhere. Alternatively, she may remember the pain

Left: Her signals of attraction include direct eye contact, her leg-cross and knee-point towards him, her hand on her thigh, and the fact she has turned her chair so her torso faces him directly. He signals his interest in her by lowering himself so that their eyes meet on a similar level. His open body posture, palm display, knee-point and hand-point are further clues, and his invasion of her personal territory is done in such a manner as to seem neither aggressive nor domineering.

Right: Her arm is crossed in front of her, protecting herself from his dominant display and more threatening invasion of her intimate personal space zone. His palm down on her desk top, his angle of torso lean, his pointing hand and his eyes glancing down at her breasts are all less attractive than his previous position.

of ending a previous relationship, or a friend's warning about the new object of her desire. Conflicting internal and external messages create the uncomfortable condition of simultaneous attraction towards and repulsion from the potential source of attraction or hurt. And while the intellectual argument rages, internally the woman's body may be providing her with a complicated chemistry of physical desire. A man is just as likely to undergo similar internal conflicts. Sometimes people find themselves in the dilemma of thinking they don't find someone attractive while simultaneously being inexorably drawn towards them. This double bind will inevitably be comunicated nonverbally. Bear in mind, however, that with time thoughts and feelings can change.

SELF-DISCLOSURE

When we first meet people, it is as if we present a full-sized cardboard cut-out of ourselves, held at arm's length in front of us. On this board we display numerous trivial facts and figures about

ourselves: our tastes in food and music; our politics; our work. As time passes we begin the vital work of self-disclosure; inch by inch we pull the cardboard cut-out to one side to reveal more about the 'real' us. As with the 'scratch my back and I'll scratch yours' exchange, so we do the same with information. The game is a familiar one; given the chance many children will play, 'I'll show you mine, if you show me yours' – a developmental milestone of non-verbal sexual communication. Adults do the same, but with more intellectual information. Reveal too much too soon – like the stranger on the bus who pours out horrendous become bogged down. Trust is central to successful seduction, sex and love. It is also the gold dust of non-verbal communication. Trust in your instincts, trust in your senses, trust your inner skills to understand and translate the sometimes furtive, near-invisible messages another person is

personal problems to the unwilling, impromptu counsellor – and the listener is put off; reveal too little, especially in the face of intimacies revealed to you, and your listener will feel cheated and hurt. So be sensitive, and keep the scales balanced.

You need not always initiate the next move in these exchanges, but be prepared to do so if things giving you. If you detect reservation or doubt in your partner's face or body, respond. Pull back a bit, be less pushy, empathize and take your time. Men especially are often guilty of rushing their prospective partners. They expend so much energy thinking about what is going to happen in the near future that they forget to enjoy what is happening in the present. The tiny subtle steps that our bodies go through as we grow more trusting of and attracted to someone else are deliciously exciting; each one deserves to be savoured to the full and nurtured with care. Each experience in building a

Left: Imagine you are at a party observing these guests across the room. The couple to the left are sending out numerous positive courtship and sexual readiness signals. These include their mutual comfort at being in each other's intimate space zone, the mirroring of their crossed and touching legs, her hand resting on his chest, their mutual gaze, his arm resting on the back of the sofa as if about to come down around her shoulders, her torso turned towards him. By contrast the other couple appear totally uninterested in each other; nearly all their signals are closed and non-communicative. Are they perhaps a couple who have just had an argument? Perhaps they have never met and are both extremely shy; perhaps they find each other incredibly attractive but are so confused by the intense feelings they are experiencing that they can hardly bear to look at each other.

relationship, especially in the very early stages, is profoundly enhanced if we stay in the present instead of dashing ahead or worrying over memories of earlier partnerships .

LIVING FOR THE PRESENT

Concentrate on the here and now. Assimilate all the messages that your five senses are giving you. Use your eyes with care; they are the principal tools with which to put into practice all the knowledge you have learned from this book. Read the world well and wisely; ask yourself a constant stream of questions; pay great attention to detail. Scan the people you meet like a high-tech robot, noting every body position and the signals those

bodies are sending out to others and to you. What do they seem to be saying? What has their body dialogue got to do with you? And what are their eyes communicating to you? Eye-to-eye contact is one of the most intimate of all exchanges. Draw deeply on the information that other people's eyes reveal to you, and allow them to look into your mind in return. Extend an unconditional welcome to your would-be lover: your courage will bring rewards for both of you.

Listen with care to all the sounds that people make; note breathing rate; listen for calmness in the voice, confidence in the tone and the animation and articulation of speech. Take notice of the speed at which people speak and, most importantly, listen well to their words, for they will help you test the theories you will have been building based on the non-verbal communication you have already observed. Listen carefully to what they say; it helps to find out who they really are, what they believe in, what they like and dislike and what makes them tick. Speech reveals our thoughts with an added definition that will serve to support or contradict the non-verbal language.

Pay attention to the words a person speaks whatever their body may say. Even though a person may be apparently giving you every possible signal of sexual interest, if on approach the person says 'No', you must respect the words. Being able to see the reality of non-verbal sexual signals does not give you the right to act upon those signals unless the other person gives you conscious and verbalized consent.

USING ALL THE SENSES

If intimacy is to ensue in an 'all systems go' situation all your other senses will be of great importance. Taste is a sensuous thing, a vital ingredient in love-making, and it plays a central role in the non-verbal sexual bonding between people. Smell, too, as we have seen, can be the most important non-verbal signal that our bodies send to each other. Get to know the taste and smell of your partner's body; familiarity will be comforting, arousing and bonding. Explore your own taste and smell, too; have courage, be daring and you may well be pleasantly surprised.

Slow down and luxuriate with your partner, enjoy the sensation of skin-on-skin touch. Two people in love who are really connected to each other can hold entire conversations without murmuring a word: the slightest touch by a gentle hand against an arm can speak volumes; a hand on a back, a small stroke of the leg or knee, the

enquiring caress of a cheek, the massaging hand on the back of a stiff neck, a teasing touching of feet, a squirm-inducing tickle or a mischievous hand slipped into a pocket. We all need touch for comfort and reassurance. In our adult lives we all have a need for physical comfort and 'hug therapy' is healing for all of us.

THE POWER OF TOUCH

With increased confidence and knowledge and the practical application of your non-verbal sexual skills, you will feel really good giving and receiving, offering and asking for quality touch with your lover. Touch between two people changes everything; wherever two bodies touch, both

Left: A man and a woman arrive simultaneously at a market stall. They find each other mutually attractive and begin a series of courting rituals. He stands facing her, his body slightly inclined towards her, his head tilted teasingly to one side; he is smiling broadly and with direct eye contact, his hands are in his pockets in a mild crotch point and his feet are pointing towards her. She is laughing at something he has said and returning his eye gaze. Initially they stand in the social space zone, just beyond each other's outstretched touch, but close enough to talk without raising their voices. Below: He moves into her personal space zone, stands straighter and animates his conversation with his right hand. She turns to face him but brings her hands together in front of her in a slightly protective position. She leans slightly towards him, maintaining eye contact. Right: They move into each other's intimate space zone. He makes her really laugh, her arms open up and she moves forward. She touches his right arm and in doing so signals to him that she finds him as attractive as he clearly finds her.

parties are connected to each other physically, taking the dynamic between those two people on to a whole new dimension of interaction. Sensitivity to the timing of touch can mean the difference between increased intimacy or, alternatively, withdrawal and rejection. Tune in to the signals that your partner's body and your own are sending, and act upon them thoughtfully. In the times when one of you is feeling a need for more space you should be sensitive to and understanding of this need. It does not mean you are being rejected – it is simply that each of us has times when we feel like withdrawing and isolating ourselves from a lover. Use your touch to reassure, and remember that when the person close to you needs extra room to breathe withholding touch is as loving an action as extending it.

ATTENTION TO DETAIL

In the short story 'Hunted Down', Charles Dickens remarked on the importance of paying careful attention to every detail of a person's non-verbal communication when he wrote 'An observer of men who finds himself steadily repulsed by some apparently trifling thing in a stranger is right to give it great weight. It may be the clue to the whole mystery. A hair or two will show where the lion is hidden. A very little key will open a very heavy door.' In the same way, as we have seen, there are numerous very subtle yet potent sexual non-verbal signals that men and women can send to each other; the power of a glance; the accidental brush of a hand; the touch of a foot.

Stage 1. Courtship Readiness

1 Eyes brighten
2 Skin around the eyes smoothes out
3 Muscles become toned
4 Body more erect
5 Complexion reddens

Stage 2. Positioning for Courtship

1 Personal space encroached on,
   then merging
2 Stance leaning towards each other
3 Orientation: bodies angled at 45°
4 Speech: tone and volume lower

Stage 3. Actions of Appeal and Invitation

1 Preening
2 Leakage
3 Autoerotic touching
4 'Accidental' touching
5 Deliberate stroking;
   push-me-pull-you tactics
6 Flirtatious glances; gaze holding
7 Head cocking
8 Rolling the pelvis
9 Leg crossing and uncrossing to
   expose the thigh
10 Hand on hip
11 Wrist and palm exposure
12 Protruding breasts
13 Slow stroking of upper thigh and
   side of thigh with fingers
14 Softer facial expression
15 Verbal invitations / flattery /
   suggestion / confirmation
16 Open smile
17 Echoing and mirroring

Situations change from moment to moment. People are endlessly fluid in their movements and moods; their body language is changing all the time. Half

Above: An ambiguous arm-cross position. His body is quite slumped over and his arms are resting on his raised knee, apparently forming a barrier. However, this is not a closed position because the torso and chest are still unprotected.

Right: The contrast in the body language of these men on a sofa at the edge of a dance floor is marked. The man on the left seems uncommunicative, unattractive and cold, even hostile. The man in the middle is so over-enthusiastic he looks as if he is about to spring out of his seat. His open body posture and grinning face might be offputting to a potential dancing partner. The man on the right looks most comfortable. His arm position has changed from the one shown above to an open wrist grip. His relaxed expression and open leg stance suggest that he is confident and approachable.

the pleasure of using knowledge of sexual signalling at a practical level is seeing how you can
interact with people and make their body language
change, for example, from negative and closed off
to warm and inviting. Most interactions include

for advice and second opinions, and for protection.
We can feel very vulnerable walking into a place
alone. Especially in the case of women, groups
protect us from being seen to be alone and therefore from being assumed to be single and to be

mixed messages. Both parties are testing the water,
not committing themselves until they are sure of
where the other person stands.

Social convention, influenced by the primal and
tribal competitive nature of 'hunting for a mate',
encourages men and women to 'go out on the
hunt' in bands of the same sex. Our confederates
are there for mutual support and encouragement,

therefore searching for a lover or a 'good time'.

As custom still puts the onus on men to make
the initial move, a single man is faced with a
dilemma if he wants to talk to one of a pair of
women. The tactics of approach will obviously
depend on the body language messages being
exchanged. It may be that the solitary man is
receiving clear invitations to initiate an interaction,

they have noticed. However, if one leaves the other to go off to the toilet or to buy another drink, make a phone call and so on, this may be the time to make a positive move. If the woman to whom the man is attracted has left the room, he can approach her friend and establish contact with her. He can even say he is interested in her absent friend and enquire if the pair are waiting for male company to arrive or if he might join them. Many mistakes and embarrassing blunders are made due to careless observation: for example, if the friend has gone to the bar the man will start off on the wrong foot if he suggests that he might buy drinks. The woman will obviously reject his offer, the initial verbal exchange will have invoked a negative word and an opportunity to make acquaintance may have been lost.

Someone sitting alone who keeps glancing at his or her watch and the door is almost certainly waiting for a date, and nervous body language will indicate 'first date' jitters. If a person is already focusing emotional attention onto someone any non-verbal or verbal sexual approach will almost certainly be warded off. If, on the other hand, a man is still nervously glancing at his watch after an hour and a half do you assume he has been stood up, rush in to reassure him and thereby risk the wrath of his hurt pride, or do you assume that

in which case he may like to approach and talk to both women as a polite opening move. It is always worth observing the interaction between the two (or more) women: is it confident and flirtatious, or are they locked deep in conversation about something serious? In the latter case, an approach from anyone is going to be rebuffed as unwelcome. Does one of the pair appear to be doing all the talking or making all the decisions? If so, does the man talk to the dominant one or the shy one first? Circumstances will determine the most appropriate action, and correct timing of the initial approach is vital. It is common for women to go off to the ladies' room together to gossip generally, to preen themselves, check clothing, repair make-up and apply perfume, and sometimes to discuss the men

Above left: At first glance the woman appears to be annoyed by her workmate's advances. His arm against the pillar is an aggressive territorial display, his torso leaning towards her is an invasion of her space zone. She averts her face and folds her arms, yet her left foot points to him and she is lifting her breasts with her arms.

Right: Now she flirts openly with him, smiling broadly, preening her hair, her hand on her hip. He is more relaxed and less intense, touching her gently on the wrist.

his apparent 'waiting' behaviour is actually nervous displacement activity and that for the last hour and a half he has been wishing someone would come and talk to him?

These questions are typical of the informal analysis you can carry out in your head when reading non-verbal body language. Remember, never judge a book by its cover; appearances can be deceptive. Err on the side of risk in this game. How many wonderfully attractive men or women have you looked at and immediately assumed to be attached, saying to yourself something like, 'They are absolutely gorgeous . . . they must be with someone'? People make assumptions all the time, but you should never assume anything. Use your eyes and brain to amass all the non-verbal information that is there for the taking. It costs nothing, it is distinct, and it is the principal mode of human communication. Words do matter, of course, but they are secondary and come late in the overall scheme of things. The ability to interpret body language gives you a head start in establishing what communication is likely to follow.

Use your ears to their full capacity as well. Names can be easily overheard; plans for the evening, or even who a person may fancy, might be revealed in conversations between friends. Draw on your intuition. What kind of gut feeling do you get? Is there a warning voice in your head you should listen to?

As with most disputes in life, there is always room for a negotiated compromise between passion-driven impulse and intellectual caution. The very ambiguity of non-verbal sexual signals permits us a high degree of flexibility because we need not commit ourselves to verbal opinion. For example, if we spy someone to whom we are highly attracted, then on closer inspection or

after verbal exchange find we are less taken with them, any previous gestures of interest can be altered, withdrawn or denied, verbally or non-verbally, without embarrassment to either party. As the social psychologist Judy Gahagan wrote, 'Non-verbal communication is a language adapted for hint and innuendo.'

We have seen throughout this book how the mutuality and synchrony of non-verbal signals leads to more pleasing and rewarding interaction. What follows is an overview.

BE REALISTIC

If you spend an hour gazing deeply into the eyes of your favourite pin-up on your bedroom wall before going out for a drink, you are inevitably going to be disappointed by the looks of the people you will encounter at your local pub. Do not set yourself up to fail – be realistic and be practical. It is true that the visual impact we make on people has a profound effect on their first impressions of us and that great looks are of course an obvious asset in non-verbal attraction. But rest assured that great beauty also brings with it its own problems, and is not a prerequisite for romantic success. Personal qualities such as a sense of humour, intelligence, manners, consistency, tolerance, sensitivity, trust, courage, loyalty, sincerity, optimism and honesty far outshine glamorous looks in their worth.

TACTICS

A little-known phenomenon recently uncovered by social psychologists is that if you do someone a favour you tend to find that person more attractive! So if you ask someone to do a favour for you and they agree willingly, they are likely to subsequently find you more appealing. Apparently, this is because we assume we must be doing the person a favour because they deserve our help. In our unconscious mind this makes the person appear more attractive to us. At a conscious level, it makes us feel good to do something helpful or pleasing for someone else and if we feel good in another person's company we attribute the good feeling partly to them. In addition, under the agreement of 'You scratch my back and I'll scratch yours', we venture good things, emotional and physical, consciously and subconsciously, in the hope of reciprocation.

Timing a strategic withdrawal is an art that takes practice. When you have made a significant non-verbal contact with another person, the most exciting tactic you can employ is to retreat. This sends the message, 'I may be interested, but then again I may not. Why not find out? Chase me.' This fans the flames of curiosity. Do not play too hard, but beware of losing your nerve too soon. Really skilled practitioners of non-verbal sexual signalling know just as well when their presence is not welcome as when it is.

Right: As we fall in love our faces begin to glow, the bags under our eyes decrease, we frown less, we smile more, our skin blooms and we can look younger, our eyes have a certain dreamy gaze about them, and our general expression changes so markedly that other people remark upon it. As the psychoanalyst Sigmund Freud put it, 'When I set myself the task of bringing to light what human beings keep hidden within them by observing what they say and what they show, I thought the task was a harder one than it really is. He that has eyes to see and ears to hear may convince himself that no mortal can keep a secret. If the lips are silent he chatters with his fingertips; betrayal oozes out of him at every pore.'

INNER CONFIDENCE

Wisdom knows and research confirms that people who feel themselves to be attractive are correspondingly rated by others as being attractive. A happy confidence in our ability to attract others has the benefit of making us appear more relaxed and therefore facially more youthful; it allows us to smile a natural symmetrical smile, and helps us to respond more positively to feedback from others. If you are feeling confident in your ability to attract the opposite sex, you are less likely to assume the person smiling across the room must be merely signalling to someone right behind you – a supposition which would be to discount your own substantial worth and potential as a partner as well as your physical appeal.

THE WHOLE PICTURE

BE ASSERTIVE

Possessing the quality of assertiveness can benefit us all. We need to be capable of being assertive when we are turning away unwanted advances because this will enable us to control the anxiety

your words clear. If necessary keep on repeating yourself over and over. Do not give in to guilt-trips, manipulation or blackmail. Shield your body with your arms. Reduce your face movements to a minimum. Be very firm but do not employ attacking, malicious or cruel tactics.

which frequently besets us in social encounters.

The following simple instructions can help you to relax in nerve-racking moments, especially when you are saying 'No'. Remember to keep breathing steadily. Put more energy into breathing out than breathing in. Keep both feet flat on the ground and stand tall. Maintain eye contact while saying 'No'. Try to avoid sending ambiguous signals, like smiling while saying no. Keep your voice even and

If you are rejected by another person, withdraw with style. Accept 'no' for what it means. At the moment it is spoken it is someone's truth and you must respect it. People may change their minds, they may not. Your self-respect will be enhanced by calmness and clear thoughts even in the face of bitter disappointment. Never resort to using physical violence: it brings nothing but hate, regret, disharmony and hurt.

THE MOST ATTRACTIVE COMBINATION

A combination of mature and immature features seems highly desirable as it implies a rounded personality. The key is to work on enhancing the best qualities you already have, and then to acquire other qualities which may not at first seem obvious but which through observation and imagination you can develop with a little thought and practice. Men and women have much to learn from each other. Men can become more socially skilled with women by observing them and learning from them. Women are more skilled than men at non-verbal communication. Clear, concise, honest communication leads to better mutual understanding and attraction. Men who acquire some feminine communication skills will be more successful in attracting a mate. Women who adopt some of the more masculine features of sexual communication can equally find that their ability to attract and keep the man of their desires is enhanced.

BE TRUE TO YOURSELF

If, when you begin talking to your new acquaintance, you discover that he or she hates your favourite piece of music with as much passion as you love it, you might be tempted to do an about turn, betraying both the bond you are forming and your musical taste in the interests of trying to be what you think you are required to be.

At best this has the effect of lowering your self-esteem and at worst it makes you appear fickle, insincere, dishonest, or unreliable – all things that are sure to put off a potential lover. Instead, enjoy your differences, credit each other with firm convictions and the potential to widen musical horizons, and continue exploring in order to find more compatible albums in your collections.

We instinctively accept the old adage that like attracts like, in some respects at least. We want people to like the same things as we do because mutuality and compatibility make us feel that we are less likely to be rejected and more likely to be loved for ourselves. Similarity breeds content, but opposites attract. Both apparently contradictory statements are true: there are almost as many celebrated couples who look alike physically as there are apparent mismatches, for example between very tall, beautiful women and short, dumpy men.

What matters is this: do not limit yourself by buying into the myth that you have to be very attractive physically in order to have romantic success. The desire for instant gratification of lust may rely on the superficial 'red flag' of the model Adonis or Aphrodite, but like any false god's promise, the pleasure is always temporary, and is followed by a feeling of emptiness or regret, and a longing for something of more depth. The real riches of any relationship are not the static ones of looks and physique but the ongoing 'dynamic' ones of communication, conversation, tactics, touch, intimacy and, of course, body language.

AND FINALLY . . .

* Try not to blow it when you open your mouth: mind what you say.
* Good manners are not out of date: always pay a compliment but don't go over the top.
* Don't give away too much too soon. Secrets can be smothering, discretion alluring
* Learn to listen well; gain information.
* Use your memory. Do not forget a name you have just been told.
* Speak clearly, so that there are no misunderstandings.
* Tell no lies. They will always catch you out later, when it might really matter.
* If you are blessed with a sense of humour, use it; laughs always win hearts. If you are not, do not try too hard to be funny – it could ruin everything.
* Modesty wins more respect than big mouths most days.
* Don't get paralytically drunk and then expect anyone sober to find you remotely attractive.
* Don't be too keen.
* Never discuss previous lovers during early stages.
* Always carry paper and a pen that works!

BIBLIOGRAPHY

Alicke, M. D., Smith, R.H., & Klotz. 'Judgements of physical attractiveness; the role of faces and bodies.' *Personality and Social Psychology Bulletin* 12 (1986), 381–9.

Ardrey, R. *The Territorial Imperative.* Collins, London, 1967.

Argyle, M. *Bodily Communication.* 2nd edition, Methuen, London, 1988.

Argyle, M. *Social Interaction.* Methuen, London, 1968.

Argyle, M. *The Psychology of Interpersonal Behaviour.* Penguin Books, 1967.

Argyle, M., Furnham, A. & Graham, E. J .A. *Social Situations.* Cambridge University Press, 1981.

Argyle, M. & Henderson, M. *The Anatomy of Friendships.* Penguin Books, 1985.

Aronson, E. *The Social Animal.* 2nd edition, Freeman, San Francisco, 1976.

Axtell, R. E. *Gestures.* Wiley, New York, 1991.

Berscheid, E. 'Interpersonal Attraction', in *Handbook of Social Psychology,* edited by G. Lindzey & E. Aronson. Random House, New York, 1985.

Bettleheim, B. *The Uses of Enchantment.* Knopf, New York, 1976.

Birwhistell, R. L. *Introduction to Kinesics.* University of Louisville Press, 1952.

Birwhistell, R. L. *Kinesics and Context.* Allen Lane, London, 1971.

Brownmiller, S. *Femininity.* Paladin, London, 1986.

Brun, T. *The International Dictionary of Sign Language.* Wolfe, London, 1969.

Cahoon, D. D. & Edmonds, E. M. 'Male-female estimates of opposite sex first impressions concerning females' clothing styles.' *Bulletin of the Psychonomic Society* 27 (1989), 280–1.

Carnegie, D. *How to Win Friends and Influence People.* Angus & Robertson, Sydney, 1965.

Cohen, D. *Body Language in Relationships.* Sheldon Press, London, 1992.

Colton, H. *The Gift of Touch.* Putnam's, New York, 1983

Cook, M. & Wilson, G. (eds), *Love and Attraction.* Pergamon Press, Oxford, 1979.

Critchley, M. *Silent Language.* Butterworth, London, 1975.

Dale-Guthrie, R. *Body Hot-Spots.* Van Nostrand Rheinhold, New York, 1976.

Danziger, K. *Interpersonal Communication.* Pergamon Press, Oxford, 1976.

Davitz, J. R. *The Communication of Emotional Meaning.* McGraw-Hill, New York, 1964.

Dodson, B. *Sex for One.* Harmony Books, 1987.

Duck, S. *Human Relationships.* 2nd edition, Sage, London, 1992.

Ekman, P. *Darwin and Facial Expression.* Academic Press, New York, 1973.

Ekman, P. & Friesen, W. *Unmasking the Face.* Prentice Hall, London, 1975.

Ekman, P. *Telling Lies.* Norton, 1985.

Fast, J. *Body Language.* Pan, London, 1970.

Gahagan, J. *Social Interaction and Its Management.* Methuen, London, 1984.

Givens, D. *Love Signals.* Crown, New York, 1983.

Goffman, E. *Interaction Ritual.* Allen Lane, London, 1972.

Goldman, W. & Lewis, P. 'Beautiful is good: evidence that the physically attractive are more socially skilful.' *Journal of Experimental Social Psychology* 13 (1977), 125–30.

Hall, E. T. *Silent Language.* Doubleday & Co, New York, 1959.

Hall, E. T. *The Hidden Dimension.* New York, 1966

Hargreaves, D. J. & Colley, A. M. (eds). *The Psychology of Sex Roles.* Harper & Row, New York, 1986.

Hartley, P. *Interpersonal Communication.* Routledge, London, 1993.

Henley, N. M. *Body Politics: Power, Sex and Non-verbal Communication.* Prentice-Hall, 1977.

Hess, E. H. 'Pupilometrics' in *Handbook of Psychophysiology*, edited by N. Greenfield & R. Sternbach. Holt, Reinhart & Winston, New York, 1972.

Hinde, R. A. (ed). *Nonverbal Communication*. Cambridge University Press, 1972.

Hinton, P.R. *The Psychology of Interpersonal Perception*. Routledge, London, 1993.

Hopkins, C. *Man Hunting*. Angus & Robertson, 1990

Hopkins, C. *Girl Chasing*. Angus & Robertson, 1991

Huston, T. C. 'Ambiguity of Acceptance, Social Desirability, and Dating Choice.' *Journal of Experimental Social Psychology* 9 (1973), 32–42.

Kahn, E. J. & Rudnitsky, D. *Love Codes*. Signet, 1992

Kalick, S. M. 'Physical attractiveness as a status cue.' *Journal of Experimental Social Psychology* 24 (1988) 469–89.

Key, M. R. *Non-verbal communication: A Research Guide and Bibliography*. Scarecrow Press, New Jersey, 1977.

Kleinke, C. L. 'Gaze and eye contact; a research review.' *Psychological Bulletin* 100 (1986), 78–100.

Kurtz, R., & Prestera, H. *The Body Reveals*. Harper & Row, New York, 1984.

Lamb, W. *Body Code*. Routledge & Kegan Paul, London, 1979.

Lewis, D. *The Secret Language of Success*. Bantam Press, London, 1989.

Liggett, J. *The Human Face*. Constable, London, 1974.

Lont, C. M. & Friedley, S. A. (eds). *Beyond Boundaries: Sex and Gender Diversity in Communication*. George Mason University Press, 1989.

Lyle, J. *Body Language*. Hamlyn, London, 1991.

Maslow, A. H. *The Farther Reaches of Human Behaviour*. Viking Press, New York, 1971.

Masters, W. H. & Johnson, V. E. *Human Sexual Response*. Little, Brown, Boston, 1966.

Morris, D. *Intimate Behaviour*. Jonathan Cape, London, 1971.

Morris, D. *Manwatching*. Jonathan Cape, 1977.

Mortimer, J. (ed). *Great Law and Order Stories*. Penguin Books, London, 1990.

Pease, A. *Body Language*. Sheldon Press, London, 1984.

Poyatos, F. *New Perspectives in Nonverbal Communication*. Sage, London, 1983.

Quilliam, S. *Sexual Body Talk*. Headline, London, 1993.

Sigall, H. & Landy, D. 'Radiating beauty: effects of having a physically attractive partner on person perception.' *Journal of Personality and Social Psychology* 28 (1973), 218–24.

Simpson, J. A., Gangestad, S. W. & Lenna, M. 'Perception of physical attractiveness: mechanisms involved in the maintenance of romantic relationships.' *Journal of Personality and Social Psychology* 59 (1990), 1192–1201.

Smith, M. J. *When I Say No I Feel Guilty*. Bantam, 1975.

Symons, D. *The Evolution of Human Sexuality*. Oxford University Press, 1979

Wainwright, G. R. *Body Language*. Hodder & Stoughton, London, 1985.

Walster, E., Aronson, V., Abrahams, D. & Rottman, L. 'Importance of physical attractiveness in dating behaviour.' *Journal of Personality and Social Psychology* 4 (1966), 508–16.

Westland, G. *Current Crises of Psychology*. Heinemann, London, 1978.

Weitz, S. (ed). *Nonverbal Communication*. Oxford University Press, 1974.

Wolf, N. *The Beauty Myth*. Vintage, 1990.

AUTHOR'S ACKNOWLEDGEMENTS

Many people have helped directly and indirectly with this book. I owe great thanks in particular to the following, each of whom in their own way has been invaluable. Firstly, to Simon Naudi for introducing me to psychology, and to Professor Brian Foss, for believing in my potential to become a psychologist by offering me a place to study at London University. Special thanks to Jenny Wallace Cumio for keeping

me sane during first year statistics lectures with endless laughs, without which I would never have qualified. A big hug and endless thanks to Adrian Lancashire, grammar guru and master-observer of human behaviour, for teaching me to use my eyes wisely and for using his to read and correct the script so meticulously. To Andy Evans for his inspired common sense and psychological insight. To David Harries, for teaching me so much about human communication and the subtle art of running training groups. To Ann Rickey, for teaching me about honesty and the value of truth in relationships. To Sian Facer at Reed Illustrated for believing in the book and to Diana Vowles for her work as editor. To Colin Gotts for his masterful photgraphs. To Carole Waecthler, for typing the script, against the odds, from my illegible scrawl. To Vianne Fahmi, for teaching me the incredible dangers of falling in love with physical perfection. To Michael Perring and Anita Bingeman for providing me with the heavenly sanctuary of 'La Tuque' in Bordeaux, where I wrote this text in such tranquillity. All my love and thanks to my dear Mother and my family for their endless support. And finally, to my many friends for their hilarious anecdotes of love's labours lost, intimate body language disasters and outrageous non-verbal successes with members of the opposite sex, for teaching me the art of flirting and for validating the saying that 'Love Is Action'.

PUBLISHER'S ACKNOWLEDGEMENTS

COMMISSIONING EDITOR SIAN FACER
ART EDITOR KEITH MARTIN
ART DIRECTOR JACQUI SMALL
EDITOR DIANA VOWLES
PRODUCTION CONTROLLER ANTONIA MCCARDLE

PHOTOGRAPHY

Photographer COLIN GOTTS
Styling MARIANNE COTTERILL
Hair and makeup LIZ PUGH, GARY AHRENS

Wigs on pages 92-93 kindly lent by Trendco,
229 Kensington Church Street, London W8

*The publishers would also like to thank Agnès B,
111 Fulham Road, London SW3 for the loan of
clothes; The First Yacht Club, Temple Pier,
London WC2; ballerinas Louise Spink and Tanya
Grafham at The Arts Educational School.*